LOOKING-GLASS

*Michael Sutton
and
C S Whitcomb*

BROADWAY PLAY PUBLISHING INC
New York
www.broadwayplaypublishing.com
info@broadwayplaypublishing.com

LOOKING-GLASS
© Copyright 1983 Michael Sutton and Cynthia Mandelberg

All rights reserved. This work is fully protected under the copyright laws of the United States of America. No part of this publication may be photocopied, reproduced, stored in a retrieval system, or transmitted, in any form or by any means, electronic, mechanical, recording, or otherwise, without the prior permission of the publisher. Additional copies of this play are available from the publisher.

Written permission is required for live performance of any sort. This includes readings, cuttings, scenes, and excerpts. For amateur and stock performances, please contact Broadway Play Publishing Inc. For all other rights please contact B P P I as well.

Cover art by Barry Moser

First edition: January 1983
This edition: May 2017
I S B N: 978-0-88145-002-6

Book design: Marie Donovan
Play text set in Baskerville by BakerSmith Type, N Y C
Printed and bound in the U S A

ENTERMEDIA THEATRE
Under the Direction of
Joseph Asaro
Executive Director

David Secter
Creative Director

DAN FAUCI, JOSEPH SCALZO & THE ACTORS INSTITUTE
in association with
Frances T. Hillin, Allen Schoer and Entermedia
present

LOOKING-GLASS
by
MICHAEL SUTTON
and
CYNTHIA MANDELBERG

with
JOHN VICKERY
as Lewis Carroll

and

RICHARD CLARKE
MELANIE HAGUE
NICHOLAS HORMANN
TARA KENNEDY
ROBERT MACHRAY
INNES-FERGUS MC DADE
RICHARD PETERSON
MITCHELL STEVEN TEBO
GEORGE TYNAN

and
TUDI WIGGINS
as Mrs. Liddell

Scenery by	Lighting by	Costumes by
JOHN ARNONE	FRANCES ARONSON	JEANNE BUTTON

General Management
ROBERT S. FISHKO

General Press Representatives
THE MERLIN GROUP, LTD.

Directed by
DAVID H. BELL

CAST
(in order of appearance)

Charles Lutwidge Dodgson	John Vickery
Reverend Dodgson	Richard Clarke
Chaplain MacDougal	Robert Machray
Robinson Duckworth	Nicholas Hormann
William Hayden	Richard Peterson
Jenkins	Mitchell Steven Tebo
Dean Liddell	Richard Clarke
Alice	Tara Kennedy
Mrs. Liddell	Tudi Wiggins
Miss Prickett	Innes-Fergus McDade
Boy	Mitchell Steven Tebo
Josiah Gibbs	Robert Machray
Young Woman	Melanie Hague
Agnes	Tara Kennedy

Opening date: June 14, 1982

PLACE: Oxford, London, and the imagination of Charles Dodgson
TIME: The years 1855–1875

PRONUNCIATION GUIDE

"slithy"	SLY-thee
"gyre"	same g sound as in "gimble"
"Cheshire"	rhymes with "pressure"
"Godstow"	sounds like "God's toe"
"Liddell"	rhymes with "fiddle"
"Deanery"	"Dean'ry"
"Edinborough"	EDDin-bruh
"Dodgson"	DOD-son
"Lutwidge"	LUTT-widge

Act One

(There is no curtain. The stage is in darkness.)

VOICE: 'Twas brillig, and the slithy toves
    Did gyre and gimble in the wabe . . .

(Lights come up to reveal a frozen tableau: a group of Victorians under black umbrellas on a train platform. Three trunks are piled center. The umbrellas obscure the faces of everyone except a young man seated on one of the trunks, a carpetbag and a stack of books beside him.

He is CHARLES LUTWIDGE DODGSON *and it is he whose voice we have just heard. In his early twenties, slender, with sensitive features, he is dressed conservatively even for the era. Using a book as a lap-desk, he writes as he speaks.)*

DODGSON: All mimsy were the borogroves,
    And the mome raths outgrabe . . .

(Suddenly, the lights alter, and the others unfreeze. One closes his umbrella and turns to DODGSON. *He is the* REV. CHARLES DODGSON, *a formidable figure of fifty-four, the image of an upstanding man of God. He holds a train ticket in one hand, the folded umbrella in the other.)*

REVEREND DODGSON: Charles!

(A look of apprehension comes over the younger DODGSON'S *face. He stops writing.)*

REVEREND DODGSON: It is time for us to make our farewells. Your train will be here shortly. Here's your ticket and your umbrella.

DODGSON: *(Taking ticket and umbrella)* So s-soon?

REVEREND DODGSON: This must be an exciting time for you, my boy. Leaving the nest at last to take your place in the world . . .

DODGSON: Yes. Father, I really d-don't think I should be—

REVEREND DODGSON: I'm proud of you, Charles. We always knew you would do well, of course, but to become a lecturer at Oxford University, the finest in our land . . .

DODGSON: Yes, well, I haven't w-won the lectureship yet, Father. I've only been n-n-nominated—

REVEREND DODGSON: *(Seeing what he's been writing)* What's this? Hard at work already? *(Taking it, reading)* "Twas brillig and the . . . slithy . . . sleethy . . . " *(Sternly)* Charles!

DODGSON: It's j-just something for the children . . .

REVEREND DODGSON: Charles, I thought we had been over all this.

DODGSON: Yes, father . . .

REVEREND DODGSON: Such childish whimsy was all very well at home, but you are a man now, entering a world where such nonsense has no place.

(Train sounds.)

REVEREND DODGSON: Beware of giving in to such frivolity, Charles. Beware of indulging in idle pastimes . . .

(A golden glow bathes the scene. The elder DODGSON again freezes in time, his son's demeanor changing suddenly.)

DODGSON: Beware the Jabberwock, my son!
       The jaws that bite, the claws that catch!
     Beware the Jubjub bird, and shun
       The frumious Bandersnatch!

ACT ONE LOOKING GLASS 3

(The sound of the train grows louder.)

DODGSON: And as in uffish thought he stood,
   The Jabberwock, with eyes of flame,
   Came whiffling through the tulgey wood,
   And burbled as it came!

(As the puffing, snorting sound of the steam engine becomes deafening, he strikes at the "Jabberwock" with his umbrella.)

DODGSON: One, two! One, two! And through and through
   The vorpal blade went snicker-snack!

(The engine sighs as the train comes to a halt.)

DODGSON: He left it dead, and with its head
   He went galumphing back.

(DODGSON resumes his former position. The lights alter and the scene unfreezes.)

CONDUCTOR'S VOICE: York . . . Birmingham . . . Oxford . . . London . . . ! Now boarding!

REVEREND DODGSON: Well Charles. The time has come.

DODGSON: F-father, wait! It's not right for me to l-leave you like this. The children . . .

(Sound of the train starting up. REVEREND DODGSON and the station begin to move off.)

REVEREND DODGSON: You'll see them all when you visit on holidays.

(Train sound grows louder.)

DODGSON: But they'll be older! They'll have changed!

REVEREND DODGSON: *(Shouting to be heard)* What?

DODGSON: *(Loud)* It won't be the same!

REVEREND DODGSON: *(Disappearing into the wings)* Goodbye, Charles! Look after yourself!

(The train sounds are replaced by the chimes of Oxford. The people at the station have been transformed into university students, crisscrossing the stage around DODGSON. *A diminutive, rabbity* CHAPLAIN *scurries on, almost colliding with him.)*

CHAPLAIN: Oh. Excuse me. Late for chapel. Oh dear.

(He dashes off. DODGSON's *rooms form themselves around him. They are simple and sparsely furnished, a framed looking glass at the back. Dust-covers shroud the furniture. His trunks and carpetbag stand center.* DODGSON *examines his surroundings with resignation, a condemned man surveying his cell. He approaches the trunks and opens one, taking out a framed photograph. Looking at it, his features soften, his mind transported to another world, another time.*

His reverie is interrupted by two young men who appear in the doorway and enter without knocking. The taller of the two, ROBINSON DUCKWORTH, *wears a rumpled tweed suit and a cap which he does not remove. He carries a book in one hand, a half-eaten roll in the other.*

The other, WILLIAM HAYDEN, *is slightly neater in appearance. At first we do not see his face, as his nose is buried in yet another book, a half dozen more under his arm.)*

DUCKWORTH: *(Perching on the desk)* You see, Hayden? Follow the trail of the wild Oxford don, and you trap him in his lair. Dodgson, I take it?

DODGSON: Y-yes . . . how did you know?

DUCKWORTH: *(Exhibiting the book-plate)* "Ars Ex Libris." Pardon my Latin. *(Snapping the book shut, he tosses it to* DODGSON*)* You left a trail of them across Tom Quad.

DODGSON: Oh . . . thank you . . .

HAYDEN: *(Holding up a book)* Theology?

DODGSON: M-mathematics. Christ Church.

DUCKWORTH: *(Shaking his hand)* Robinson Duckworth, Latin, Trinity. *(Indicating his friend)* Willaim Hayden, Physics, Exeter. Bearing up under your new student vows?

(HAYDEN *gives* DODGSON *the rest of his books.*)

DODGSON: *(Confused)* Uh . . . yes . . . I suppose . . .

DUCKWORTH: *(Sitting on trunk)* Well, frankly, my dear fellow monk, it's driving me mad. No courting till after commencement. I tell you, Dodgson, a dozen young ladies weep nightly over that particularly cruel rule. Hayden will bear me out—won't you, old man?

HAYDEN: *(Who has been surveying the room)* No room.

DODGSON: I beg your p-pardon?

HAYDEN: You've got three trunks but only two cupboards. It defies the laws of Physics.

DUCKWORTH: *(Eating his roll)* One young lady actually took to her bed in grief.

HAYDEN: Turned out to be influenza.

DUCKWORTH: *(Ignoring him)* But fortunately, no less than three of them have sworn to save themselves until my release.

HAYDEN: Yes, that solves it. *(Grabs the dust cover off a chair, tips a trunk on end and drapes the cloth over it.)* You'll have to use the third trunk as a tea-table.

DODGSON: But I'm afraid I haven't any t-tea.

HAYDEN: That's your problem, old man.

DUCKWORTH: *(Looking at his pocket watch)* It will be time for tea in exactly twenty-eight minutes and fourteen seconds.

DODGSON: *(Putting the books on his desk)* Yes, well, I am afraid I h-have rather a lot to do, so if you will excuse me . . .

DUCKWORTH: I see you're admiring my watch.

HAYDEN: *(Sitting on second trunk, near* DUCKWORTH*)* He was doing nothing of the sort.

DUCKWORTH: And well you might, as it happens to be the finest chronometer this side of the Zuyder Zee. Made in Geneva, solid gold case, seventeen rubies. It was bequeathed to me . . .

HAYDEN: In a dart game.

DUCKWORTH: Before I was converted.

DODGSON: V-very nice.

DUCKWORTH: Nice? It's the finest, most accurate timepiece in all of Oxford! It never loses more than a second a day.

HAYDEN: You've gotten him started now.

DUCKWORTH: Pay no attention to him. He's only jealous because *his* watch doesn't run at all.

DODGSON: And therefore keeps better time. If you'll excuse me, I really ought to be . . .

DUCKWORTH: *(Standing)* Wait a minute! What was that you said . . . about his watch keeping better time than mine?

DODGSON: Well, it's . . . no . . . no, I shouldn't have m-mentioned it . . .

HAYDEN: *(Crosses to* DODGSON—*sits on desk)* No, you don't. You can't get out of this one.

DUCKWORTH: That's right. Explain yourself.

DODGSON: *(Reluctant but surrounded)* Well, if . . . if your watch loses a second a day, it won't come right again for . . . one hundred and eighteen years. Agreed?

DUCKWORTH: Well, I . . .

DODGSON: Now suppose his watch is stopped at, say, three o'clock. How many times a day does three o'clock come round?

DUCKWORTH: Twice, but . . .

DODGSON: Exactly. So his watch is correct twice a day, while yours is only correct once every hundred and eighteen years.

HAYDEN: My word! We have discovered a logician.

DUCKWORTH: Wait a moment. How do you know when three o'clock comes round? Hayden's watch won't tell you.

DODGSON: Very simple. You just keep your eye on Hayden's watch, and the very moment it is right, it will be three o'clock.

HAYDEN: *(Laughing)* Why, of course! I always *knew* I had the better watch!

DUCKWORTH: I've suddenly developed the most piercing headache . . .

DODGSON: Oh, d-dear, I am sorry. I knew I shouldn't have . . .

HAYDEN: *(Crosses R, looks in trunk)* What's this? *(He pulls it out: a large, flat, round object)*

DODGSON: Really, it's nothing.

DUCKWORTH: But it looks so intriguing. Rather like a round billiard table.

DODGSON: It is.

DUCKWORTH: Circular billiards! Where did you get it?

DODGSON: It's my own invention.

HAYDEN: An inventor, too!

(HAYDEN *finds the cue and three balls and sets up the game.*)

DUCKWORTH: *(Taking off his coat, and handing it to* DODGSON*)* It so happens, my good man, that you have before you the Billiard Wizard of Birmingham. *(Takes the cue stick away from* HAYDEN*)*

HAYDEN: *(Sitting right of board)* Former billiard wizard.

DODGSON: But you see the angles are somewhat different from those of a . . .

DUCKWORTH: Stand away.

(DUCKWORTH gets down on the floor and sets up a shot.)

HAYDEN: You'll forgive me for withholding my wagers.

DUCKWORTH: *(As he misses)* There's a trick to it . . . there's got to be . . . *(He lines up another shot)*

DODGSON: Not exactly a trick . . . a mathematical formula . . .

DUCKWORTH: *(Missing again)* Bit rusty.

HAYDEN: *(Having found the portrait on the desk)* Hello. Who are they?

DODGSON: My brothers and sisters. *(To DUCKWORTH)* Would you like me to . . . uh . . .

DUCKWORTH: Off the red.

HAYDEN: Big family.

DUCKWORTH: *(Shooting and missing)* Dash it all!

DODGSON: *(Getting down on the floor and taking the cue stick)* Here, let me show you. *(DODGSON lies on his belly on the floor. DUCKWORTH and HAYDEN crouch down to study the angle.)* You have to take the degree of curvature into account. Watch this. *(He hits a perfect shot.)*

DUCKWORTH: *(Taking cue back)* By jove, give me that thing.

(A contemptuous-looking young man, JENKINS, appears in the doorway smoking a large pipe. He surveys the scene.)

JENKINS: Well. Where else to find wayward children but in a playground.

DUCKWORTH: *(To HAYDEN)* Is it my imagination, or did the weather suddenly take a turn for the worse?

JENKINS: Missed you two in chapel this morning. Most interesting sermon on the book of Job. "He openeth also their ear to discipline and commandeth that they return from iniquity." Chapter 36, verse 10. I'm sure the Proctor will be relieved to learn that your absence was not due to illness.

HAYDEN: *(Sits on trunk)* Hope you didn't have too much difficulty tracking us down, Jenkins. Or do you use a bloodhound these days?

(Seeing DODGSON for the first time, JENKINS studies him narrowly.)

JENKINS: Who are *you*?

DODGSON: I . . .

DUCKWORTH: *(Putting down his cue, rises, takes his coat back and puts it on again)* How very rude of me. Charles Dodgson, Wilfrid Jenkins.

DODGSON: *(Offering hand to JENKINS)* I'm very p-pleased to meet you.

JENKINS: *(Ignoring hand)* You shouldn't be. I am your opponent for the lectureship. *(Producing an envelope)* Here. I was instructed to deliver this to you by Dean Liddell.

DODGSON: *(Taking envelope and opening it)* Thank you.

(DODGSON crosses to desk, reading.)

HAYDEN: What's in it?

DODGSON: *(Opening it)* An invitation to dine at the Dean's house on Thursday.

HAYDEN: Not bad, old man.

DUCKWORTH: Hayden, I'll give you five to three odds that it's Dodgson who wins the lectureship.

JENKINS: *(Icily)* I think it only fair to inform you, Dodgson, that as far as the lectureship goes, you haven't the remotest chance of winning. You see, I have it wrapped up. Everyone at Christ Church knows better than even to try. Only a fool would apply for it. Therefore, I assume you will withdraw from the competition.

DODGSON: I'm afraid you c-can't assume that.

JENKINS: What do you mean?

DODGSON: You see, I d-didn't apply for the lectureship, I was nominated. Therefore, by your definition, I can seek it without being a fool. *(Crosses down right, thinking to himself only out loud)* In fact, the only logical deduction you can draw from the statements: (a) everyone at Christ Church knows better than even to try, and (b) only a fool would apply for it, is that . . . *you are the only fool in Christ Church.*

DUCKWORTH: *(Awed)* My word!

HAYDEN: Good show!

JENKINS: Unless you tread carefully, Dodgson, you may lose more than just the lectureship. *(He starts for the door.)*

DUCKWORTH: Jenkins. Remember our scripture for the day: "How much less man, that is a worm?" Job. Chapter 25, verse 6.

(With an angry glare at DUCKWORTH, JENKINS storms out up left. DODGSON starts after him, concerned. DUCKWORTH and HAYDEN burst into laughter.)

HAYDEN: *(Crossing up left to DODGSON)* Dodgson, you're a wizard! We've been insulting Jenkins for years and he never left a room that fast.

DODGSON: *(Crossing toward DUCKWORTH)* I d-didn't mean to insult him. But you see, logically . . .

DUCKWORTH: I've never seen him so upset. He was positively foaming at the gills.

HAYDEN: Did you see how red his face got? First evidence we've had that he has blood in his veins.

ACT ONE LOOKING GLASS 11

DODGSON: *(Sitting on trunk)* I'm . . . I'm afraid I made rather a bad impression on him . . .

DUCKWORTH: *(Going back to the billiards)* Oh, don't worry about him. You made a marvelous impression on us, that's the important thing.

(As DUCKWORTH *lines up another shot, the lights dim to a spot on* DODGSON. DUCKWORTH *and* HAYDEN *freeze.)*

DODGSON: *(Coming down front into spot)* Dearest Father: I miss the children terribly. It has only been three days since I left home, yet it seems like three months. At this rate it will be seven and a half years until Christmas, and they all will have forgotten me. I am so homesick it is hard for me to study. I know how much it means to you to have a scholar in the family—but if all else fails, there's always Skeffy and Ned. Love to everyone. Your dutiful son, Charles.

(Lights rise on the Deanery room. Facing DODGSON *are the rabbity* CHAPLAIN, *standing L, and* DEAN LIDDELL, *a portly middle-aged gentleman standing in front of a sofa UC.)*

DEAN: Well, Dodgson. Here you are. You know Chaplain MacDougal.

DODGSON: Yes.
                    (Simultaneously)
CHAPLAIN: No.

(Pause)

DODGSON: No.
                    (Simultaneously)
CHAPLAIN: Yes.

DEAN: Good. I shall be watching your work here with particular interest. Your father and I were classmates, you know. Come, sit down.

DODGSON: Thank you.

(They all sit, the DEAN *on the sofa center,* DODGSON *and* CHAPLAIN *on either side.)*

DEAN: Well, now.

(Awkward pause.)

DODGSON: You have a m-most lovely . . .

(Simultaneously)

CHAPLAIN: I was telling the Dean . . .

(They both stop embarrassed.)

DODGSON: I beg your pardon.

CHAPLAIN: Not at all. Do go on.

DODGSON: N-nothing really. It wasn't very imp-p-portant.

DEAN: Ah . . . Dodgson, I can't help noticing that . . . ah . . . when you speak, you exhibit a certain . . . ah . . .

DODGSON: Hesitation?

DEAN: Exactly.

DODGSON: Yes, sir. Fortunately, it doesn't affect me all the t-t-time.

DEAN: Yes, well I'm glad to hear that. Much as we might wish it otherwise, I'm afraid one of the inherent duties of a lectureship is . . . ah . . . lecturing.

DODGSON: Yes, sir.

DEAN: Now as to the question of your religious commitment . . .

DODGSON: *(Rises)* You need have no apprehension on that p-point, Dean Liddell. I intend to follow my father into the ministry.

(A lovely little girl enters and peers around as if looking for something. She is ALICE LIDDELL, *the* DEAN's *eight-year-old daughter. The* DEAN *and* CHAPLAIN, *sensing her presence, turn and see her. She stops down center facing* DEAN*)*

DEAN: Alice, you must learn to knock before entering a room. Your father is having a talk with some of his friends.

ALICE: *(Going upstage to* DEAN*)* But Father, it's Dinah. I can't find her anywhere.

DODGSON: *(Entranced)* Might I request an introduction?

DEAN: What? Oh, very well. Dodgson, Alice. Alice, Dodgson.

(ALICE *crosses to* DODGSON *and curtsies politely.)*

DODGSON: How do you do?

ALICE: *(Unimpressed)* Hello. Father, I've got to find Dinah.

(ALICE *crosses to corner DR.)*

CHAPLAIN: I am afraid we've not seen tail nor whisker of your little cat, my dear.

DEAN: *(Sits on couch)* There you are. Now, run along.

DODGSON: *(Standing, going to her)* Perhaps I might be of some assistance. Could you give me a description of this Dinah?

(The lights go dark except for a pool of light surrounding DODGSON *and* ALICE. DEAN *and* CHAPLAIN *freeze.)*

ALICE: She's a cat and she's disappeared.

DODGSON: I see . . . a disappearing cat. She isn't by any chance a Cheshire cat, is she?

ALICE: A Cheshire cat?

DODGSON: Yes. Does she grin, for instance?

ALICE: Cats don't grin.

DODGSON: On the contrary. All of them can and most of them do.

ALICE: Well, she might grin sometimes... when no one's looking.

DODGSON: And about the disappearing... which part of her was it that disappeared first? The ears or the tail? Or did she vanish all at once in a puff of smoke?

ALICE: *(Enjoying his nonsense)* I don't know. I wasn't watching.

DODGSON: Ah, always a grave mistake where Cheshire cats are concerned. I once knew one that disappeared quite slowly, beginning with the tail and ending with the grin. It was a most curious thing, you know, to see a grin without a cat instead of the other way round.

(Lights rise on the scene as MRS. LIDDELL *enters, a pleasant Victorian matron.* DEAN *and* CHAPLAIN *unfreeze. All the men rise and face her.)*

MRS. LIDDELL: Here you are, Alice. You shouldn't be intruding on your father and his friends, my dear.

DODGSON: Oh, but it has been a most d-delightful intrusion, Mrs. Liddell.

MRS. LIDDELL: You are too kind, Mr. Dodgson. *(Calling off)* Miss Prickett! Alice is in here!

*(A plain-looking woman—*MISS PRICKETT*—enters DL and holds at the door. The moment she sees* DODGSON, *she becomes self-conscious).*

PRICKETT: Come along, Alice. Your sisters are already upstairs.

ALICE: *(Crossing to center)* I can't go upstairs. I have to find Dinah.

MRS. LIDDELL: Do as you're told, my dear. You have lessons to do.

ALICE: I finished my lessons. I want to stay here.

DODGSON: I'm sure we'd all enjoy Alice's company a few minutes more.

MRS. LIDDELL: You're very kind, Mr. Dodgson, but I wouldn't dream of troubling you . . .

DODGSON: Oh, no trouble at all. Her presence would be quite welcome.

DEAN: Oh, all right. Let her stay a while.

MRS. LIDDELL: Very well. If you'll excuse us. Miss Prickett?

(MRS. LIDDELL exits DL.)

PRICKETT: Yes, Ma'am. Good evening, gentlemen.

(She exits. ALICE pulls a footstool center and sits on it. The men resume their seats.)

DEAN: Well . . . ah . . . Dodgson, what do you think of this so-called Indian Rebellion? Nasty business, eh?

DODGSON: *(His eyes on ALICE—then, coming to, looking at DEAN)* What? Oh . . . yes, I suppose . . .

(Awkward pause. The DEAN and the CHAPLAIN appear confused by DODGSON's interest in ALICE.)

CHAPLAIN: You know, Dean Liddell, all of Oxford is talking about your plans for a new belfry. Isn't that true, Mr. Dodgson?

(But DODGSON is too preoccupied to respond.)

CHAPLAIN: Mr. Dodgson . . . ?

DODGSON: What? Oh. *(Rises)* You'll have to pardon me, gentlemen. I'm afraid I'm not really very good at c-conversation. In fact, I've been told I'm rather b-boring.

DEAN: My dear boy . . .

CHAPLAIN: *(At the same time)* Why, you're nothing of the sort.

DODGSON: Th-thank you.

(Another long pause. The CHAPLAIN *fidgets restlessly.)*

CHAPLAIN: *(At last, rising)* Well, I, ah . . . really must be going, I'm afraid.

DEAN: *(also rising)* Come, come, Alfred, surely you can stay for dinner? We're having your favorite soup.

CHAPLAIN: *(Standing)* Really? No. More pressing duties, you know. *(Crosses to* DODGSON, *who also rises, and shakes his hand)* It was a . . . uh . . . a pleasure to meet you, young man. I hope that we see each other again . . . occasionally . . .

DODGSON: Thank you, sir. Good-night.

(The CHAPLAIN *exits DL.)*

DEAN: I'll see you to the door. Excuse me for a moment, won't you, Dodgson?

DODGSON: Certainly. Take as long as you like.

(The DEAN *exits DL.* ALICE *crosses DL after her father. When the others are gone, she turns back to* DODGSON.*)*

ALICE: Do you have a cat?

DODGSON: *(Sits)* Alas, no.

ALICE: *(Disappointed)* Oh.

*(*DODGSON *gets an idea, turns so he is sitting on the chair with his back to her. He pulls out his handkerchief and twists it around his hand.)*

DODGSON: I do have a mouse, however.

ALICE: You do?

DODGSON: *(Still fooling with handkerchief)* Let's see . . . he was here somewhere . . .

ALICE: *(Excitedly)* You brought it *with* you?

DODGSON: Well, he was with me when I came in . . .

(From his folding and tying, the handkerchief starts to take on the form of a white mouse, which his fingers manipulate from the inside, two corners making the ears.)

ALICE: There he is!

DODGSON: I do hope you're not afraid of mice. Their feelings are quite easily hurt, you know.

ALICE: Oh no, not me. Prickett thinks they're dreadful, but I think mice are very nice.

DODGSON: Ah, we're in luck, Mouse. This is a young lady with good sense and a kind heart.

(The "mouse" listens to DODGSON, *then looks at* ALICE *and nods approval.)*

ALICE: May I hold him, please?

DODGSON: Certainly.

(He makes the mouse-puppet climb onto her shoulder, where it sniffs at her ear. ALICE *giggles delightedly.)*

ALICE: What's his name?

DODGSON: Oh, he doesn't have one. He's just a common pocket-mouse, you know.

ALICE: I should introduce him to Dinah.

(The "mouse" scurries frantically back to DODGSON *and hides under his coat.)*

ALICE: *(Dismayed)* Oh, dear . . .

DODGSON: I'm afraid Mouse is rather undone by the mention of c-a-t's.

ALICE: I'm very sorry, I'm sure. Mouse . . . dear Mouse, do come out. It's really quite safe.

(The "mouse" looks out, shakes his head, and disappears again.)

ALICE: Perhaps if I do a recitation . . .

DODGSON: Perhaps. Mice are very fond of rhymes, you know.

ALICE: They are? Let me see . . . *(Curtsies and faces front)*
   Come out, dear Mouse . . .
   Into my house . . .

(The "mouse" pokes his head out.)

DODGSON: I do believe it's working.

ALICE: Stay for tea,
   We'll . . . we'll eat a flea!

(It comes out onto DODGSON's knee.)

DODGSON: We'll talk of anything you please,
   And never mention c-a-t's.

   (It dances on his knee)

   Do a dance upon my knees,
   I'll find for you a piece of cheese!

(Taking the "mouse," which is still on DODGSON's hand, ALICE holds it to her cheek.)

ALICE: I love him!

(Lights dim to a spot on DODGSON. ALICE freezes. DODGSON goes DC to spot.)

ACT ONE — LOOKING GLASS

DODGSON: Dear Father: I may have been overly pessimistic in my last letter. Kindly disregard. *(He considers the handkerchief mouse fondly. A second spot reveals a well-dressed thirteen-year-old* BOY *sitting on a straight-back chair center, taking laborious notes and sniffling.)*

BOY: Next problem.

*(*DODGSON *continues looking wistfully at the mouse.)*

BOY: Mr. Dodgson. *(No response)* Mr. Dodgson!

*(*DODGSON *is jarred from his reverie. Lights rise full to reveal that they are back in his rooms.)*

DODGSON: *(Turning to look at* BOY*)* Hmm . . . ?

BOY: May I have the next problem, please?

DODGSON: Yes, of c-course. *(*BOY *sneezes.)* Are you certain you wouldn't rather continue this some other time? You do seem to be suffering from rather a bad cold.

BOY: I believe we still have twenty minutes to go, Mr. Dodgson.

DODGSON: *(With a sigh)* Quite so . . . *(Crosses above* BOY, *playing with the "mouse")* The next problem . . . If a mouse trapped in a cage with one hundred and eighteen bars can gnaw through one bar every twenty minutes, how long will it take him to escape?

BOY: I thought this was supposed to be algebra.

DODGSON: *(Snapping out of it, taking handkerchief off hand and putting it in his pocket.)* Very well. If y varies directly as x, and y equals thirty when x equals five, find y when x equals fifteen. Is that stated plainly enough for you?

(The BOY *snorts.)*

DODGSON: *(To audience)* The little thing grunted in reply. *(He addresses the* BOY *directly.)* Don't grunt. It's not at all a proper way of expressing yourself.

(The BOY *snorts again.* DODGSON *examines his face closely, but the* BOY *does not seem to notice.)*

DODGSON: There could be no doubt that it had a very turned-up nose, much more like a snout than a real nose; also its eyes were getting extremely small . . .

(The BOY *continues snorting in a way that has now become decidedly pig-like.)*

DODGSON: If you're going to turn into a pig, my dear, I'll have nothing more to do with you!

BOY: *(Turning back into himself as he figures)* . . . y equals ninety!

*(*DUCKWORTH *and* HAYDEN *rush in carrying a large crate with a basket balanced on top.)*

DODGSON: Here! Wh-what are you—?

(They set the crate downstage of the settee, standing back to admire it. DODGSON *crosses above* BOY, *standing between the* BOY *and the crate.)*

DUCKWORTH: Yes, Yes, I think so. *(To* HAYDEN*)* Don't you?

HAYDEN: Perfect.

DODGSON: What's all this then?

DUCKWORTH: *(Sitting on settee, up left of crate)* Found you a new tea-table, old man. How do you like it?

BOY: Mr. Dodgson, am I to understand that my lessons have come to a premature . . .

HAYDEN: *(Taking a teapot out of the basket)* Tea?

BOY: . . . conclusion?

ACT ONE   LOOKING GLASS   21

(The BOY *picks up his satchel as if to leave.)*

DUCKWORTH: *(Rummaging through* DODGSON's *cupboards)* Look what I found . . . muffins!

(They begin laying out the things they find on the top of the crate, setting it up for tea.)

DODGSON: *(To the* BOY*)* What? oh . . . n-no . . . no . . .

HAYDEN: *(To* DUCKWORTH*)* How about some jam?

DUCKWORTH: Just the thing.

DODGSON: *(To the* BOY*)* Well, perhaps they have . . .

BOY: *(Standing)* Very well, but I find your behavior highly . . .

HAYDEN: *(Finding the jam)* Found it. *(He tosses the jar in the air.* DODGSON *catches it as it sails dangerously close to the* BOY's *head.)* Catch!

BOY: . . . irregular!

DODGSON: Sorry . . .

DUCKWORTH: Not really first-class jam, but it'll do.

HAYDEN: The butter's good, anyway.

BOY: *(Picks up satchel, crosses UL, turns back to* DODGSON*)* And I intend to make a full report of this incident to Mama! *(Stamps his foot)*

DODGSON: *(Irritated beyond endurance)* Get out!

(He does, hastily. DUCKWORTH *and* HAYDEN *sit at the crate and begin helping themselves to the food.)*

DUCKWORTH: Thought you were fond of children, old man.

DODGSON: I am. Some children.

*(*DODGSON *puts the* BOY's *chair back behind the desk.)*

HAYDEN: Seemed like a well-behaved lad to me.

DODGSON: Insufferable little pig . . . I mean, *prig*.

DUCKWORTH: Well, don't let him upset you. Sit down and have some tea.

(HAYDEN *sits right of* DUCKWORTH.)

DODGSON: I'm afraid I d-don't have time for tea.

DUCKWORTH: Oh, that's all right. It isn't tea-time.

DODGSON: *(Turns to them, still at desk)* Look, fellows, I d-don't mind your being here, but I'm supposed to be studying Euclid.

HAYDEN: Not at all, old man. Make yourself at home.

DODGSON: *(Referring to the crate)* Where did you g-get that thing, anyway?

DUCKWORTH: What? You mean this? Found it outside your door.

DODGSON: My door?

HAYDEN: Sitting smack in the middle of the hall. Caused quite a jam.

DODGSON: *(Inspecting it)* It's a delivery for me! *(Then, excitedly)* I wonder . . .

(DODGSON *goes back to the desk, hunting for something to open the crate—finds a T-square, disregards it.*)

HAYDEN: I thought you didn't have time.

DUCKWORTH: *(Gesturing with teaspoon)* Know what your problem is, Dodgson? You haven't learned to deal properly with time.

HAYDEN: Cream?

(DUCKWORTH *holds the spoon out of his cup and watches* HAYDEN *pour cream.* DODGSON *grabs* DUCKWORTH's *teaspoon and uses it to pry open the crate. There isn't a moment's pause in the dialogue.)*

DUCKWORTH: Please. I mean, no one else studies as hard as you do. Look at Jenkins.

HAYDEN: If you care to.

DUCKWORTH: He wants the lectureship every bit as badly as you.

HAYDEN: Worse.

DUCKWORTH: But even *he* finds time for relaxation.

HAYDEN: Pulling wings off flies, things like that.

(DODGSON finally pries open the front of the crate and looks inside while the tea party continues on top.)

DODGSON: It is! It's the camera I ordered!

DUCKWORTH: *(looking)* Camera! Latin word, you know. Means "chamber."

(They lean over the table to have a closer look, as DODGSON pulls the camera and bag of accessories out of the crate.)

DUCKWORTH: I've read about these things, but this is the first one I've ever actually set eyes on.

HAYDEN: *(Holding up a lens)* Fascinating . . . everything's all upside down and backwards. *(To DUCKWORTH)* Care for a look—

DUCKWORTH: I? A student of Divinity? Touch an instrument of the devil? Give it here.

(HAYDEN gives DUCKWORTH the lens, but DODGSON takes it from him.)

DODGSON: P-please. It isn't a toy, you know. It's an extremely delicate instrument.

(DODGSON *sits with the lens on end of settee beside* HAYDEN. DUCKWORTH *crosses upstage of the settee, holding above them.*)

HAYDEN: What are you going to do with it?

DODGSON: *(Studying the lens)* I intend to m-make a thorough study of its f-functions.

DUCKWORTH: And here *I* thought it was for taking photographs.

HAYDEN: Really, Duckworth, sometimes you can be positively dim.

DUCKWORTH: *(Stands R of settee)* I think it would be rather jolly to have a photograph of oneself in one's prime—before the wrinkles and gray hair and paunch set in. One could actually preserve oneself at one's absolute best—noble expression, sunlight in one's hair—and keep it that way forever. *(Sitting R of settee)* With a photograph you can stop time itself.

(HAYDEN *and* DUCKWORTH *freeze.*)

DODGSON: *(Thoughtfully, rising, facing front)* " . . . stop time . . . "

(*The lights alter quite suddenly.* DUCKWORTH *pops open a tophat hidden behind the basket and puts it on. He and* HAYDEN *become caricatures of themselves as the Mad Hatter and March Hare respectively.*)

DUCKWORTH: *(Standing)* Move down!

DUCKWORTH and HAYDEN: *(Ad lib)* No room! No room!

(DUCKWORTH *and* HAYDEN *both stand and move down toward* DODGSON, *who has to cross front and take* DUCKWORTH's *old seat on the right of the sofa. When they finally all sit again,* DUCKWORTH *is in the middle of the sofa.*)

DUCKWORTH: *(Pulling out his watch)* What day of the month is it?

HAYDEN: *(Looking at* DUCKWORTH's *watch)* The fourth.

DUCKWORTH: Ah! A hundred and eighteen years wrong! I told you butter wouldn't suit the works.

HAYDEN: It was the *best* butter.

DUCKWORTH: *(Shaking the watch)* Yes, but some crumbs must have got in as well. You shouldn't have put it in with the bread knife.

(HAYDEN *dips the watch into his full teacup, by raising the cup under as it hangs from* DUCKWORTH's *hand.)*

HAYDEN: *(Looking gloomily at the watch)* The *best* butter, you know . . .

DUCKWORTH: *(To* DODGSON, *taking his watch up out of* HAYDEN's *cup)* I daresay *you've* never even spoken to Time.

DODGSON: Perhaps not.

DUCKWORTH: *(Puts arm around* DODGSON *and stands, pulling* DODGSON *up beside him)* Ah! That accounts for it. Time and I quarreled last March—just before *he* went mad, you know— *(They look at* HAYDEN *who suddenly looks quite mad)* —and ever since that, he won't do a thing I ask! It's always six o'clock now . . . always tea-time . . .

(DUCKWORTH *and* DODGSON *sit again,* DUCKWORTH *flattens his hat into his lap so that it is no longer visible. The lights return to normal, just as suddenly as before.)*

DODGSON: *(Standing)* That's it!

DUCKWORTH and HAYDEN: *(Simultaneously)* What?

DODGSON: *(Gathering up his camera and plates)* It's going to be six o'clock forever! Duckworth, you're an absolute genius!

DUCKWORTH: *(To* HAYDEN*)* What did I say?

(*Blackout. Spot comes up on* DODGSON *standing DR with the camera set up facing UL.* DODGSON *faces front and speaks to the audience.)*

DODGSON: May twenty-seventh. First session photgraphing Alice and her sisters. We went down to the river bank. The light was quite excellent. Alice saw a rabbit.

(Lights rise. MISS PRICKETT sits beside a large picnic basket and an open parasol. ALICE stands beside her facing the camera ready to be photographed. DODGSON goes under the blackcloth at the back of the camera and sets up the shot.)

DODGSON: Are you ready? Now don't move . . .

(ALICE and PRICKETT freeze. DODGSON emerges from under the cloth and speaks to the audience.)

DODGSON: *(Front)* What a marvelous invention. With a camera, one is actually capable of capturing one moment—one perfect, golden afternoon—and holding it in the palm of one's hand. The light just so through the new leaves . . . the way the wind stirs a tiny curl against a child's cheek . . . the impossible brilliance of the mid-day sun on a starched white pinafore . . .

(The scene resumes.)

DODGSON: Very good. You may relax.

ALICE: *(Crossing to DODGSON)* Can't we do something different? I'm tired of just standing.

DODGSON: Why, surely you don't think we came all the way down here with all this heavy equipment just to take photographs of ordinary little girls. I want pictures of gypsies and dancers and red Indians.

ALICE: But we haven't any costumes.

DODGSON: That does present a problem, doesn't it? Well, now, I wonder where we might find some. What if we were to look in my bag, for instance?

(DODGSON hands ALICE his photography bag. She runs to PRICKETT

with it and they pull out a fancy fringed shawl. ALICE *is delighted. They freeze again.)*

DODGSON: *(Front, beside camera)* June third. Another session photographing the Liddell children. Between costume changes, they delighted in being able to run about in their favorite dress of "nothing". Alice hit upon the idea of being photographed as a fairy. The others decided to be mermaids and cherubim. As a result, we were able to produce some remarkably beautiful nude studies. As always, Miss Prickett was also present.

(ALICE *and* PRICKETT *unfreeze.)*

DODGSON: That's it. Enough for today.

ALICE: *(Draping shawl over her shoulders)* Can't we do one more? I want to be a Queen.

DODGSON: Very well, but there are too many clouds just at present. Hang on a minute and I'll think of something for us to do.

(DODGSON *goes back under the blackcloth to remove the last plate. While he is under,* PRICKETT *finds an excuse to get rid of* ALICE.)

PRICKETT: *(Taking napkin full of biscuits from basket)* Run along with the other girls and feed the ducks. (ALICE *takes biscuits and starts to go)* And don't go too near the bank.

ALICE: *(As she runs off)* Good-bye, Uncle Dodgson!

(DODGSON *comes out from under the cloth just in time to see* ALICE *run off DL. He is quite disappointed.* PRICKETT *puts the costume back in* DODGSON'S *bag and crosses to him, returning it.)*

DODGSON: Well, I must say it seemed to go well today . . . Of course a large vote of thanks is due to you, Miss Prickett.

PRICKETT: *(Blushing, she retreats to the picnic basket)* Well, I . . . I'm just doing my job, sir . . .

DODGSON: *(Looking up)* Oh, bother. Those clouds are going to be with us quite a while, I'm afraid.

PRICKETT: Would . . . would you care for something to eat as long as the children are amusing themselves . . .

DODGSON: Why, yes, that would be very nice.

(They sit side by side. PRICKETT *gives him a sandwich.)*

PRICKETT: *(Shyly)* You know, Mr. Dodgson, you're an artist, you really are. I saw some of the photographs you took of the children last week, and they are really quite beautiful.

*(*JENKINS *wanders in UR, unnoticed. At first he does not see them.)*

DODGSON: It is very kind of you to say so. I think my favorites are the ones where we dispensed with the costumes altogether. There is something so aesthetically pleasing about the unclothed human form.

PRICKETT: Why . . . yes . . . I suppose so . . .

*(*JENKINS' *eyes grow wide.)*

DODGSON: Of course you've told Mrs. Liddell . . .

PRICKETT: Well, I . . . I have been meaning to, but she's been so busy. I will, though.

*(*JENKINS *exits RC.)*

DODGSON: Good. She should be proud to have such beautiful children.

PRICKETT: Oh, I'm sure she is. *(Pause)* What were you saying . . . about the . . . human form?

*(*DODGSON *is off in his own world.* PRICKETT *hangs on his every word.)*

DODGSON: You know, I wouldn't be surprised if someday photography didn't develop into a classical art form in its own right, like oil painting or sculpture . . .

PRICKETT: Oh, how right you are, Mr. Dodgson. Why I've often thought the very same thing myself.

DODGSON: There's no reason one couldn't preserve images in photography just as well as on canvas.

PRICKETT: How forward thinking of you.

DODGSON: You know, someday I should like to photograph . . .

PRICKETT: *(Head back, lips parted)* Yes?

DODGSON: *(Standing suddenly)* Hello, there's the sun! Come along, girls! First one back to the camera gets to be a gypsy!

(PRICKETT *sighs in frustration as* DODGSON *returns to his camera. Blackout.)*

DEAN's VOICE: Disgraceful . . . absolutely disgraceful . . .

(Lights rise on the Deanery parlor. The DEAN *is pacing, muttering to* MRS. LIDDELL.*)*

MRS. LIDDELL: *(Setting down the tea things)* Is it as serious as that, Henry?

DEAN: Serious?! Our children . . . exposed to the unrestrained yearnings of a man three times their age . . .

MRS. LIDDELL: At least hear what Mr. Dodgson has to say in his defense.

DEAN: I'll give him opportunity to have his say. But if what I've been told is true . . .

(Sounds from the hallway, off.)

MRS. LIDDELL: Here they are.

DEAN: Have Prickett take the girls upstairs and bring Dodgson here.

MRS. LIDDELL: Yes, dear. But promise you won't be too harsh with him.

(DODGSON enters L.)

DODGSON: You wished to speak with me, sir?

DEAN: Yes. Yes, indeed. Come in, Dodgson.

(He does. Brief pause. The DEAN glances uncomfortably at his wife.)

DEAN: Well, ah . . . sit down, won't you? Been out using your camera again, have you?

DODGSON: *(Sitting on chair L)* Oh, yes, sir. It's been a most productive day.

(MRS. LIDDELL sits on sofa upstage.)

DEAN: Well, it's about these photographing sessions with my daughters that I wish to speak with you, Dodgson.

DODGSON: Sir?

DEAN: I am deeply disappointed in you, Dodgson.

DODGSON: In what way, sir?

DEAN: I was a student here myself. I realize how difficult it can be sometimes to keep one's romantic impulses in check, but hang it all, man, *you*, a minister's son, should know that some things are simply not done!

DODGSON: Excuse me, Dean Liddell, but what are we talking about?

DEAN: *(In disbelief)* Why, your clandestine courtship of Miss Prickett, of course!

DODGSON: P-P-Prickett?

DEAN: Of course, I understand how a young man might be thinking ahead to the day he is freed from his student vows . . .

DODGSON: *(Standing)* But, it's not true!

DEAN: Then you deny the accusation?

DODGSON: Most emphatically. Such an idea was the remotest p-possible thing from my mind, sir. I mean no insult to Miss Prickett, but . . . May I ask who has made this slanderous suggestion?

DEAN: That is of minor importance. I am releived to hear you say this, however, Dodgson. You are an honorable young man from a good family and if you say it is not true, then, of course, I believe you.

DODGSON: Thank you, sir. *(Starting for the door)* And now, if there's nothing else, sir . . .

DEAN: However, these visits with my daughters must come to an end.

DODGSON: B-b-but *why?*

DEAN: Whether the accusation is justified or not, there are those who will continue to misunderstand.

DODGSON: *(Crossing DR)* B-but it's only idle g-gossip spread by some foul-minded troublemaker.

DEAN: How does it reflect upon myself and Mrs. Liddell to have it rumored that our governess is having a romantic liaison with a student?

DODGSON: Even so, sir, I—

DEAN: And then of course there are the children to consider. What if this were to reach them?

DODGSON: *(Realization)* Please . . . You're quite right, of course. The children must be protected. I will make up some excuse to Alice . . .

(ALICE *rushes in DL and crosses to* DODGSON)

ALICE: Uncle Dodgson! I thought you'd left without saying good-bye.

DODGSON: Now, you know I could never do a thing like that. Your father and I were just having a . . . little . . . uh . . . a chat . . .

ALICE: Lorina says I'm too small to row the boat tomorrow. I'm not too small, am I?

DODGSON: Well . . . I . . .

ALICE: *(To her father)* We're going boating tomorrow, Father. All the way up to Godstow!

DODGSON: *(Kneels, facing* ALICE*)* Alice . . . I . . . I'm sorry, my dear, but it appears . . . we won't be able to go boating tomorrow after all.

ALICE: *(Shocked)* Not go!

DODGSON: *(Standing)* You see, I just remembered some important errands I have to run . . . so, I'm afraid we'll have to make it . . . some other time . . .

ALICE: But you promised! You promised we would go up the river!

DODGSON: I know, my dear . . . but sometimes it's impossible to keep one's promises.

ALICE: But you said you could do impossible things! You said you do six before breakfast every day.

DODGSON: Yes, I know, but . . .

MRS. LIDDELL: *(Who has been thinking all this out)* Henry, I'm wondering . . . perhaps Miss Prickett wouldn't mind doing those errands for Mr. Dodgson.

DEAN: Errands?

DODGSON: I b-beg your pardon?

MRS. LIDDELL: Rather than go on the boating trip, she could see to the errands; that way he could keep his promise to Alice . . . and *all* our problems would be solved.

DODGSON: *(Gratefully)* D-do you think she would?

DEAN: *(After a look from his wife)* Oh! Yes. I'm sure she would, yes. Especially when she hears there was a, ah, promise involved.

(DODGSON *is elated. The lights begin to dim except for a spot on* DODGSON *and* ALICE)

DODGSON: Do you hear that, Alice? We will go up the river, after all.

ALICE: Even if it should rain?

DODGSON: If it rains, I shall recite for you the history of the Norman Conquests, for that is the dryest thing I know.

ALICE: Then I hope it doesn't rain. I should rather hear a story.

(ALICE *takes* DODGSON's *hand and they cross C, then turn and walk slowly upstage together. Lights rise on a boat (punt) UC.* DUCKWORTH *stands holding the pole, wearing a straw hat and school scarf.* DODGSON *lifts* ALICE *into the boat, then climbs in, donning another straw hat and scarf from the boat, and taking over punting from* DUCKWORTH. DODGSON *now stands in the back of the boat with the pole,* DUCKWORTH *sits in the front of the boat, back to audience.* ALICE *sits in the center seat, L of* DUCKWORTH *facing out.*)

ALICE: Don't forget my story.

DODGSON: Alice . . . *(clears his throat)* . . . was beginning to get very tired of sitting by her sister on the bank, and of having nothing to do . . . when suddenly a white rabbit with pink eyes ran close by her.

(*The* CHAPLAIN *scurries past the boat.* ALICE *is the only one who seems to see him.*)

CHAPLAIN: Oh, dear. Oh, dear. I shall be too late . . .

(ALICE *hops out of the boat, and runs after him. They don't take any notice of her abscence.*)

DODGSON: Away she went like the wind . . .

(*The* CHAPLAIN *dashes for the other side of the stage,* ALICE *in pursuit. She is prevented from following him off by a giant mushroom—an open umbrella standing on the floor—with* JENKINS *bending over it, wearing a fez and smoking a hookah.*)

JENKINS: Who are you?

ALICE: I hardly know, sir, just at present.

JENKINS: What do you mean by that? Explain yourself . . .

ALICE: I can't explain myself because I'm not myself, you see?

JENKINS: No, I don't see. Curiouser and curiouser.

ALL: A-A-A-lisss . . .

(JENKINS *raises the umbrella above his head and circles DR and UC.* MRS. LIDDELL, DEAN, DUCKWORTH, PRICKETT *and* CHAPLAIN *all enter crossing and circling* ALICE, *ending in a group UC with their backs to the audience. In a burst of wild laughter and shouts of "No room! No room!"* DUCKWORTH *and* HAYDEN *emerge from the "clump" holding a red silk tablecloth by four corners so it appears as if there were a table under it. They circle, and stop DC by* ALICE. *They are playing the* HATTER *and the* MARCH HARE.)

ALICE: But there's plenty of room!

DUCKWORTH: Why is a raven like a writing desk?

ALICE: I . . . I don't know. Why *is* a raven like a writing desk?

DUCKWORTH: *(Idiotically)* I haven't the slightest idea! *(They laugh hysterically)*

(HAYDEN *and* DUCKWORTH *hold up two corners of the red cloth, turning the tea table into a curtain.* ALICE *runs around and sits in front of it, facing U.* DUCKWORTH *and* HAYDEN *remove the "curtain" revealing the* DEAN *as the* MOCK TURTLE, *holding the open umbrella at his back to represent his shell.* DUCKWORTH, HAYDEN *and the rest face upstage and weep as he sings.*)

DEAN: *(Weeping and singing)*
   Beautiful soup, so rich and green . . .
   Waiting in a hot tureen.
   Who for such dainties would not stoop?
   Soup of the evening, beautiful soup.

(ALICE *applauds. The* CHAPLAIN *scurries in a circle around the stage, followed by the others. They reform their "clump" facing upstage and* ALICE *is once again confronted by the tea party DR.*)

DUCKWORTH: Have some wine!

ALICE: I don't see any wine.

DUCKWORTH: There isn't any!

(HAYDEN *holds the cloth up.* DUCKWORTH *ducks behind it, going down on his hands and knees facing R.* PRICKETT—*as the Duchess—goes behind the cloth.* HAYDEN *wraps the cloth around himself like a baby blanket, as he says:*)

HAYDEN: It was the *best* butter, you know.

(PRICKETT *sits on* DUCKWORTH *as if he were a stool, taking* HAYDEN—*on his knees—in her arms as if he were her baby. He cries "waa waa" in time to her poem. She spanks him in rhythm.*)

PRICKETT: Speak roughly to your little boy.
   And bet him when he sneezes,
   He only does it to annoy
   Because he knows it teases.

(PRICKETT, DUCKWORTH and HAYDEN *disappear back into the clump.* MRS. LIDDELL *as Queen of Hearts separates from clump UL.*)

MRS. LIDDELL: He's murdering the time! Off with his head! Off with his head!

(*The clump suddenly faces front and chants in unison, the whole group crossing L together.*)

ALL: Will you, won't you, will you, won't you, will you join the dance? Woo!

(*On "Woo!" they all jump in the air, turning upstage and holding in a bunch.* MRS. LIDDELL *has countered UR and confronts* ALICE.)

MRS. LIDDELL: What's your name, child?

ALICE: *(Curtseying)* Alice, so please your majesty.

MRS. LIDDELL: Off with her head! Off with her head!

(ALICE *runs away, circling DC of clump. The umbrella suddenly opens out of the clump and* JENKINS—*lifted by* DUCKWORTH *and* HAYDEN—*appears high above her over the umbrella.*)

JENKINS: She's mad, you know.

ALICE: But I don't want to go among mad people.

JENKINS: Oh you can't help that. We're all mad here.

(*The clump breaks up, everyone circling the stage in choreographed chaos.* ALICE *runs among them as if trying to find her way. Everyone mutters or sings simultaneously, laughing, "Sooooop", "Alice!", "Will you, won't you . . .", etc.*)

(*They end with everyone spaced around the floor, suddenly still, facing front,* ALICE *DC facing out.*)

DUCKWORTH: *(singing)* Twinkle, twinkle, little bat,
          How I wonder what you're at.

ALICE: *(Overlapping)* But, where are you going?

HAYDEN: Nowhere! It's a caucus race!

DEAN: Beautiful, beautiful soup.

MRS. LIDDELL: Off with her head!

DUCKWORTH: Up above the world you fly . . .

HAYDEN: *Best* butter . . .

PRICKETT: And beat him when he sneezes.

CHAPLAIN: No time.

(Pause. Everyone holds for a moment. Together they all take one step forward, beginning to circle ALICE.*)*

MRS. LIDDELL: Off with her head!

(They take another step.)

ALICE: Am I winning?

(Another step)

JENKINS: Who are you?

(Another step)

CHAPLAIN: I'm late.

(The others begin to circle ALICE, *closing in, going faster and faster to the rhythm of the chant.)*

ALL: *(except* ALICE*)* Will you, won't you, will you, won't you, Will you join the dance?

*(*DUCKWORTH *picks* ALICE *up on his shoulder and spins her in the center of the circle as they turn faster.)*

ALL: Will you, won't you, will you, won't you,

Will you join the DANCE!

(On "DANCE!" they all stop, facing ALICE, *arms high.* DUCKWORTH *slowly lowers* ALICE *so she appears to slide down into a "rabbit hole" made by the other characters. She laughs delightedly as she falls.* ALICE *and* DUCKWORTH *slip out the back of the group and quickly take their places, unseen, in the boat. The others turn out of the circle and search for* ALICE, *calling:)*

ALL: Alice? Alice. Alice!

(They all exit. The last to disappear is the CHAPLAIN, *muttering "Late!" Just before the lights fade to blackout, we see the boat with the three sitting in it as before—*DODGSON *finishing the story.)*

DODGSON: At this they all came flying down upon her . . .

DODGSON'S VOICE: *(Continuing in the dark)* She tried to beat them off, and found herself lying on the bank, with her head in the lap of her sister, who was gently brushing away some dead leaves that had fluttered down upon her face . . .

HAYDEN'S VOICE: *(Taking over, as the lights rise)* " . . . 'Oh, I've had such a curious dream!' said Alice. And she told her sister, as well as she could remember them, all these strange Adventures of hers . . . "

(The lights reveal HAYDEN *and* DUCKWORTH *in* DODGSON's *room.* HAYDEN *is reading the last page of a handwritten manuscript;* DUCKWORTH *eats a muffin as he looks on with interest.* HAYDEN *lowers the manuscript, obviously impressed.)*

DUCKWORTH: Well?

HAYDEN: It's incredible. It's as though it were written by someone else.

DUCKWORTH: Exactly.

HAYDEN: Does he know you've seen this?

DUCKWORTH: No, I told you, I was waiting for him, and just happened onto it . . .

HAYDEN: In a closed desk drawer?

DUCKWORTH: Well, I heard him tell it on the river, so I don't see why he should mind.

HAYDEN: Hah!

DUCKWORTH: I must say I enjoyed the Hatter and his watch particularly. *(Checks his watch)* Almost two. Where can he be?

HAYDEN: When he comes in, I'll thank you to leave the talking to me.

DUCKWORTH: *(Offended)* I beg your pardon. My intention was to broach the matter in a perfectly calm and reasonable—

(There is a noise just outside the door. Panicking, DUCKWORTH tosses the muffin he is eating to HAYDEN.)

HAYDEN: No!

(HAYDEN tosses the muffin back as DUCKWORTH tosses the manuscript. They cross in midair. HAYDEN shoves the book into the desk drawer. DUCKWORTH throws the muffin back to him and HAYDEN shoves that in as well, managing to recover just as DODGSON enters, laden with photographic equipment. DUCKWORTH sits innocently on the settee. HAYDEN leans nonchalantly on the desk.)

DODGSON: *(Surprised to see them)* Oh . . . Good morning.

HAYDEN: Good afternoon.

DODGSON: *(Setting camera down behind settee)* Is it really? Already? I hadn't noticed. *(He puts down his equipment.)*

DUCKWORTH: The . . . ah . . . door was open.

DODGSON: Oh yes, of course. You know, you were right about the camera. I've managed to capture some wonderful moments of time. Would you like to see some of them?

HAYDEN: Why . . . certainly.

(DODGSON *removes a bundle of photos from his coat pocket and hands them to* HAYDEN.)

DODGSON: The lighting isn't terribly good on some of them, I'm afraid. We lost the sun behind some clouds just as I opened the shutter.

(DUCKWORTH *crosses to the desk.* HAYDEN *looks over his shoulder. As* HAYDEN *flips through the photographs,* DUCKWORTH, *looks over his shoulder.)*

HAYDEN: *(Somewhat surprised)* Why . . . these are quite marvelous, Dodgson.

DODGSON: *(Pleased)* Do you think so?

HAYDEN: Indeed I do.

DUCKWORTH: I say! Too bad she isn't a few years older, what?

HAYDEN: Honestly, Duckworth!

DUCKWORTH: I wouldn't let this one get about if I were you, Dodgson. Someone might get the wrong idea.

HAYDEN: Don't pay him any mind, old man. It's beautifully done. Rather like Rossetti, isn't it?

DODGSON: Ah, you noticed! Yes, I tried to capture his softness of line. I'm afraid it didn't turn out quite as well as I'd hoped . . .

HAYDEN: On the contrary, dear fellow—it's a masterful piece of work.

(DODGSON *crosses DS of the desk—*DUCKWORTH *nudges* HAYDEN *significantly.* HAYDEN *hooks around* DODGSON *on the left side of the desk.* DODGSON *is now surrounded.)*

HAYDEN: You're, ah, certainly a man of many talents,

Dodgson. Didn't you mention once that you write as well?

DODGSON: Did I?

DUCKWORTH: *(Casually)* Have you . . . written anything lately?

DODGSON: Nothing of any consequence.

HAYDEN: Well . . . uh . . . *what,* for instance?

DODGSON: *(Beginning to get suspicious)* Look, fellows, I'd like to stay and chat, but I must get over to the Deanery. *(Crossed to upstage of desk)* I've put together a present for Alice, and I want to give it to her before . . . *(Taking the manuscript from the desk drawer, he finds the remains of* DUCKWORTH'S *muffin resting on it.* DUCKWORTH *sheepishly takes the muffin off.)*

HAYDEN: *(Quickly)* All right, look: we shouldn't have, and we *know* we shouldn't have, but we did, and there's nothing we can do about it now, so there you are.

DODGSON: You had no right to read this. It was intended for someone else.

DUCKWORTH: Oh, come on, Dodgson . . . we're sorry for what we did, really we are, but we're all friends, aren't we? Besides, we happen to think it's blasted wonderful. *(To* HAYDEN*)* Well, we *do* . . . don't we?

HAYDEN: It's enchanting. Look, Dodgson, I have an uncle who's an editor with Macmillan's. What would you say to sending your manusript on to him?

DODGSON: *(Crossing DL of table)* No.

DUCKWORTH: What!

DODGSON: It's Alice's story—no one else's.

HAYDEN: But it's not fair, Dodgson! Think of the other children who could be charmed by your story.

DODGSON: *(Goes to settee, picks up his straw hat and scarf)* I'm quite certain that the world will survive very nicely without another children's book.

HAYDEN: All right, then, think of the money.

DODGSON: Money holds little interest for me, I'm happy to say. I am quite content with the modest income I earn from tutoring. If you will excuse me . . .

(He starts for the door UL. HAYDEN blocks his path. DODGSON gets around him and is about to exit.)

DUCKWORTH: *(Quickly)* But if it was published, you wouldn't have to tutor! You could spend more time photographing, more time writing, more time with Alice and the others . . .

(DODGSON stops in the doorway, his back to them. Pause.)

DODGSON: *(Finally)* I could?

HAYDEN: You'd have time for practically anything you liked.

DODGSON: *(Crossing DC)* They couldn't have this copy. This one is a present for Alice.

DUCKWORTH: Just copy it over, and in a few months you could give her the present of making her the most famous little girl in all England.

(DUCKWORTH and HAYDEN follow him DC. DODGSON ponders this. Lights dim to a spot on the three of them.)

DODGSON: But suppose they're not as impressed with it as you are. Suppose they d-don't publish it.

HAYDEN: Of *course* they'll publish it!

(GIBBS appears in a spot on the other side of the stage.)

GIBBS: *(Front)* I'm sorry we can't publish it.

HAYDEN: *(Also front, simultaneously with DUCKWORTH)* Uncle, what are you saying!

DUCKWORTH: *(Simultaneously with* HAYDEN*)* You can't be serious!

GIBBS: Oh, it's amusing, I'll grant you that—and well-written. But a children's book must do more than merely amuse. It must educate. It must prepare the child for the responsibilities of the adult world. In short, it must have a moral.

HAYDEN: *(To* DODGSON*)* Sorry about that, old man.

DUCKWORTH: Better luck next time.

(They start to move UC out of their spot. DODGSON *starts to go with them, then turns suddenly moving DC back into spot.)*

DODGSON: *(Front)* Mr. G-Gibbs . . .

GIBBS: Yes?

DODGSON: I beg your pardon, but I just couldn't leave without pointing out that my book does have a moral.

GIBBS: Oh, and what is that, Mr. Dodgson?

DODGSON: I'm sorry it wasn't stated clearly enough. The moral is, "Be what you would seem to be."

GIBBS: Oh?

DODGSON: Or if you'd like it put more simply: "Never imagine yourself not to be otherwise than what it might appear to others that what you were or might have been was not otherwise than what you had been, would have appeared to them to be otherwise."

GIBBS: That's nonsense, Mr. Dodgson.

DODGSON: Exactly. Silly and frivolous. And the moral to that is, childhood is the only time we have to be silly and frivolous. Why should we be in such a hurry to put an end to it?

GIBBS: I never thought of it that way before . . .

DODGSON: The moral to that is, take care of the sound and sense will take care of itself . . .

GIBBS: Mr. Dodgson . . .

DODGSON: Or if you'd like *that* put more simply . . .

GIBBS: Mr. Dodgson.

DODGSON: What?

GIBBS: You win. We'll publish your book.

DODGSON: What?

(GIBBS *exits R.* HAYDEN *and* DUCKWORTH *advance on* DODGSON *with open arms.* DODGSON *is in a state of shock. They grab him and carry him to DL corner.*)

DUCKWORTH: *(Jubilant)* Congratulations!

HAYDEN: Did you hear that, Dodgson? They're going to publish it!

DUCKWORTH: Dodgson, what's the matter?

DODGSON: *(In a sort of trance)* They're going to publish it . . .

(*Three lampposts move in. An oversized one DR, a real one with a circular bench around it C, and a smaller one UL, creating a street in forced perspective. The three turn UC and start toward the center lamppost.*)

DUCKWORTH: Wait till it gets round Christ Church that one of their foremost mathematic scholars has published a children's book.

HAYDEN: Should wake things up a bit in old Tom Quad.

DODGSON: *(Sudden realization, turning DC)* I just thought of something! My reputation!

DUCKWORTH: Your what?

DODGSON: I won't be taken seriously as a mathematician.

HAYDEN: Oh, don't be silly.

DUCKWORTH: It'll be gossiped about for a week, then it'll blow over.

DODGSON: You don't think Jenkins will use it against me for the lectureship?

HAYDEN: Well, yes, he probably will do that.

DODGSON: *(Despairingly)* My c-career is ruined before it's even started.

(They all sit on the bench C, DODGSON in center, DUCKWORTH R of him, HAYDEN L.)

DUCKWORTH: Now, wait a minute. Who says all of Christ Church has to find out about it?

HAYDEN: *(Ironic)* Oh, yes, I know a dozen Charles Dodgsons at least.

DUCKWORTH: *(Rising)* Who says it has to be by "Charles Dodgson"?

DODGSON: What do you mean?

DUCKWORTH: A *nom de plume*, old fellow.

HAYDEN: Of course! Why didn't I think of that?

DUCKWORTH: They were invented for just such an occasion.

DODGSON: Yes . . . yes, that m-might do it! What a wonderful idea! What name should I use?

DUCKWORTH: How about "Robinson Duckworth"?

HAYDEN: How about "Mister X, the Phantom Poet"?

DODGSON: *(Thinking)* What if I were to translate my Christian names into Latin?

DUCKWORTH: My specialty. Charles Lutwidge would be . . . let's see . . . "Carolus Ludovic".

HAYDEN: A bit hard to remember, don't you think?

DODGSON: I suppose you're right. Put it back into English.

DUCKWORTH: Carroll Lewis.

DODGSON: What?

HAYDEN: What happened to "Charles Lutwidge"?

DUCKWORTH: Nothing. I just translated it literally this time.

DODGSON: *(Thoughtfully, standing)* Carroll Lewis.

HAYDEN: Sounds a bit like a lady, doesn't it?

DODGSON: Lewis Carroll.

DUCKWORTH: Lewis Carroll.

HAYDEN: *(Standing as well)* Lewis Carroll.

(The realization hits them all at once.)

ALL: Lewis Carroll!

DUCKWORTH: I say, this calls for a celebration. What do you say to a pint all round, my treat?

(HAYDEN leads DODGSON DL.)

DODGSON: A pint? Oh, but I shouldn't—

HAYDEN: A *pint*? An occasion like this calls for champagne!

DUCKWORTH: *(Blanching)* Champagne? *(Checks his billfold, sighs)* Very well. Champagne it is.

DODGSON: Listen, fellows, it's awfully kind of you, but—

DUCKWORTH: *(Crossing to join them, singing)* "Champagne Charlie is my name . . . "

HAYDEN: *(Joining in)* "Champagne Charlie is my name . . .

(DUCKWORTH offers DODGSON his arm. DODGSON takes it. HAYDEN offers his too. Now they are all three arm in arm, as DUCKWORTH and HAYDEN go on with the song.)

DUCKWORTH and HAYDEN: *(Singing)* Good for any game at night, my boys! *(The three slowly turn till they face U, backs to audience)* Good for any game at night, my boys.

(They freeze for a moment—when they come back into action they sing the next line of the song, only now they are all three falling down drunk. DODGSON *now sings with them. The lamps have moved off and they are now back in* DODGSON's *room.)*

ALL: Champagne Charlie is my name.
　　　Champagne Charlie is my name.
　　　Good for any game at night my boys.
　　　Who'll come and join me in a spree.

(They collapse in a heap C on the floor of DODGSON's *room.)*

DODGSON: *(Staggers to his feet)* Fellows . . . this is the most glorious day of my life.

DUCKWORTH: Feeling better, eh, Dodgson?

DODGSON: Who?

DUCKWORTH: Oh, I beg your pardon. Thought I was talking to a friend of mine. Name of Champagne Charlie Dodgson.

DODGSON: Never heard of him.

HAYDEN: And yet, there is a resemblance . . .

DUCKWORTH: Yes, isn't there? Are you certain you're not Dodgson?

DODGSON: I'll prove it to you. Come here. *(He leads them to the looking-glass UC)* Now, look . . . look there. Does that look like this fellow . . . what's his name?

DUCKWORTH: Dodgson.

DODGSON: Does that look like this fellow Dodgson?

(They gaze into the mirror.)

HAYDEN: You know . . . I think he has a point.

DODGSON: *(Crosses to the settee—they continue to stare into the mirror for a moment after he's gone)* Course I do. Look at him . . . parts his hair on the other side and everything. *(Waves his hand airily)* Completely different person.

DUCKWORTH: By Jove, you're right. I was mistaken. My apologies.

DODGSON: Quite all right, quite all right . . .

HAYDEN: *(Crossing to* DUCKWORTH*)* But if it isn't Dodgson . . . who *is* it?

DODGSON: *(Pulls handkerchief from his pocket and hands it to* HAYDEN*)* My card.

HAYDEN: *(Reading handkerchief)* Lewis Carroll? The famous author? *(He tosses handkerchief to* DUCKWORTH *behind him, who catches it.)*

DODGSON: At your service.

HAYDEN: *(Sits beside* DODGSON*, L end of settee, offering his hand)* My dear chap, how very glad I am to meet you.

DODGSON: *(Shaking it warmly)* My pleasure.

DUCKWORTH: *(Hanky on his head, impersonating Queen Victoria, crosses and sits on R end of settee, shaking* DODGSON's *other hand)* And may we say how very much we've admired your work!

DODGSON: *(Shaking hands with both, becoming serious)* You know, I . . . I owe a great deal to you fellows. If it wasn't for you . . . I'd still be that stuffy old workaday Dodgson.

HAYDEN: Not at all, old man, not at all . . .

DUCKWORTH: Now, wait a minute—I happen to agree with him. I think we're an outstanding pair of chaps who deserve to be knighted at the earliest possible opportunity.

*(*DUCKWORTH *kneels in front of settee.)*

HAYDEN: *(Also kneeling, arms spread like a saint)* Knighted? Sainthood's the only thing good enough for us.

DODGSON: You two . . . you've shown me . . . who I really am. *(Then, confidentially)* I'm Lewis Carroll. *(Goes to the looking glass, talks to "DODGSON")* You hear that? I'm Lewis Carroll! That's who I am—Lewis Carroll! *(Singing)* Lewis Carroll is my name . . .

ALL THREE: Lewis Carroll is my/his name!
          Lewis Carroll . . .

(They can't think of a line.)

DODGSON: . . . is my name!

ALL THREE: Lewis Carroll is his name!

(They fall over each other laughing in a heap on the floor. JENKINS *appears suddenly UL, crosses to C above them.)*

JENKINS: So . . . culture comes to Christ Church at last.

(They quiet down fast.)

DUCKWORTH: You always seem to know right where to go to spoil a bit of fun, don't you, Jenkins?

HAYDEN: How do you do it?

JENKINS: It wasn't difficult. Dodgson's bellowing could be heard clear across the Quad.

DUCKWORTH: That wasn't Dodgson!

HAYDEN: Not a bit Dodgson!

DODGSON: Another fellow altogether. Latin name.

(The three of them laugh at their private joke.)

JENKINS: I do apologize then. D-D-Dodgson's the one I was looking for. You see, the Dean wants to see him.

DODGSON: *(Staggering to his feet, in shock)* The D-D-Dean?

JENKINS: In fact, he's on his way up. But why look so alarmed. After all, *you're* not Dodgson . . . are you?

(He exits L.)

DODGSON: *(Rushing to desk, trying to straighten it)* The D-D-Dean! Oh d-d-dear! What'll I d-d-do!

DUCKWORTH: D-D-Don't worry, old man. Remember: Rome wasn't burned in a day.

HAYDEN: *(Loud whisper)* Yes, it was.

DUCKWORTH: Oh. *(Staggers)* I say . . . I'd love to stick around, fellows, but I think I may be sick. *(He bolts from the room L.)*

HAYDEN: Poor Duckworth. Never could hold his— *(Turns green)* Excuse me . . . *(Rushes out after him)*

DODGSON: Hayden, wait!

(DODGSON: *grabs a few toys and inventions from his desk and rushes to the settee, dropping them as the* DEAN *enters L.)*

DEAN: Hang it all!

DODGSON: Dean Liddell!

DEAN: Some day I'd like to be able to announce a bit of good news myself. But it always seems to leak out somehow. I see you and your friends have already started celebrating—

DODGSON: Oh, no, sir—we were just . . . uh . . . what?

DEAN: Congratulations, my boy.

DODGSON: How did you know?

DEAN: What?

DODGSON: *(Confused)* Please, sit down.

(DODGSON *brings the chair from the desk to C, for* DEAN, *but* DEAN *sits on settee.*)

DEAN: *(Sits on toy, removes it, sits again)* I wanted to tell you personally because you've become rather a friend of the family. But don't think that had anything to do with it. You won the lectureship on your own merit, my boy—

DODGSON: *(Sitting in chair himself, stunned)* L-lectureship?

DEAN: Officially, of course, the announcement will not be made until tomorrow, but you should have time to prepare yourself . . . Mathematics. The study of order. A wise choice, Dodgson. In this world, we are surrounded by paradox. We live in a world where plants may eat animals, where fish can fly, where civilized men may have the blood of apes in their veins. If one were to dwell on these possibilities, he would surely go mad. They fly in the face of everything we've been taught is true. For us, the only refuge from these contradictions is Order. *(Rises, crosses behind* DODGSON, *who is drunkenly trying to follow what he's saying)* Mathematics supplies it on the purely physical level; religion, on the spiritual side. They are both essential . . . Well, I must get back to the Deanery for dinner. Be sure you have prepared your acceptance speech for tomorrow, Dodgson. And, Dodgson—your tie is undone.

(DEAN *exits L.* DODGSON *follows* DEAN *to door, then turns to fix his tie in the looking glass, trying to straighten his hair.*)

DODGSON: *(Clears his throat)* Distinguished colleagues, ladies and g-gentlemen . . . . I am honored that you chose to bestow upon me the lectures of dutyship . . . I mean the duties of lectureship . . . I am especially grateful to the little dean . . . *Dean Liddell* ! Oh bother, why can't I get it right way round. *(Pause—looking at reflection)* Of course. In the looking-glass everything comes out backwards. *(Starting over)* Distinguished colleagues . . . *(Distracted, getting an idea)* So all you have to do is find a way to go through the looking-glass. *(Suddenly struck with inspiration,* DODGSON *rushes to his desk and begins to write.)* "Alice stood on the chimney piece, though she hardly knew how she got there. And the glass began to melt away, just like a bright silvery mist . . . "

(Fade to black. A light comes up on JENKINS, *DR, crossing toward the other side. It is clear that his mood is a particularly foul one. Unexpectedly* DODGSON *enters, DL, heading in the opposite direction. Neither notices the other in time to prevent a collision DC. The books* DODGSON *has been carrying fall to the ground.)*

DODGSON: I beg your pardon . . .

JENKINS: Allow me.

(He assists DODGSON *in picking up the books. It is only then that* DODGSON *realizes who he's run into.)*

DODGSON: Oh—Jenkins—I am sorry, I wasn't looking where I was going.

JENKINS: It seems congratulations are in order.

DODGSON: How very kind of you. They say it'll be in the bookshops by the twenty-third.

JENKINS: I was referring to the lectureship.

DODGSON: Oh? Oh, yes, of course! I'd quite forgotten. Silly of me. I'm sorry there couldn't have been two of them awarded. I thank you, though, for your good wishes, and—

*(*DODGSON *picks up his scattered books during the following.)*

JENKINS: Save your thanks. I've waited a long time to tell you what I think of you, Dodgson. Taking advantage of the Dean's friendship with your father, pretending your trips to the Deanery were to see his children . . . and *now*—

(The clock chimes in the distance.)

DODGSON: Hello! Two o'clock. Sorry, Jenkins, got to run. Some other time, perhaps . . .

ACT ONE LOOKING GLASS 53

(He circles JENKINS *and exits UL.* JENKINS *finds that one of* DODGSON's *books lies forgotten at his feet. As he picks it up, annoyed, a handful of photographs falls out. He picks them up and flips through them disinterestedly . . . until he comes to the last few. His expression changes, first to one of shock, then to a victorious smirk.*

Lights dim to a spot on JENKINS. MRS. LIDDELL *appears in another spot DR.)*

MRS. LIDDELL: *(Front)* I'm sorry, Mr. Jenkins, but my husband is not at home at the moment. Is there something I can do for you?

JENKINS: *(Front)* Yes, madam, there certainly is.

(Blackout. Lights rise on DODGSON's *room.* DODGSON, *in his shirt sleeves working at his desk.* ALICE *comes in.)*

DODGSON: *(With mock sternness)* You're late.

ALICE: I'm not *very* late. I had to tell you: I read the new book all the way through, by myself!

DODGSON: *(Anxiously)* Well? How did you like it?

ALICE: It was better when you told it out loud . . .

DODGSON: *(Pantomimes being wounded in the heart)* Ah . . . I've failed!

(He collapses with his head on the desk in mock death.)

ALICE: But I like it even better than the Wonderland book.

DODGSON: *(Reviving to peek at her)* Really?

ALICE: Yes.

DODGSON: Come and tell me all about it. *(Crawls under his desk.* ALICE *meets him DS of desk and they sit on the floor together as if under the desk.)* What was your favorite part?

ALICE: Well . . . I liked the looking-glass where everything was backwards . . . and Humpty Dumpty and the talking pudding . . . but my very favorite was the White Knight!

DODGSON: Him? But he's such a dreamer. Not very practical. And a bit boring.

ALICE: I don't care. I like him best. He reminds me of you.

DODGSON: I beg your pardon!

ALICE: Tell me a new story.

DODGSON: Why, the looking-glass isn't even published yet, and you're already tired of it.

ALICE: But I'm not—I just want a new one that nobody knows but me.

DODGSON: You think I can come up with a brand new story any day of the week?

ALICE: Yes!

DODGSON: Well, perhaps . . . Do you like, um . . . Snarks?

ALICE: Yes, yes! Snarks! *(She takes his hand and drags him toward the settee, then pauses)* What are snarks?

DODGSON: Oh, they're even worse than Jabberwocks!

ALICE: Goody!

(She pulls him to the settee and they sit side by side.)

DODGSON: "Just the place for a Snark!" the" . . . um . . .
    "Bellman cried,
    As he landed his crew with care.
    Supporting each man . . ."

(He is interrupted by MRS. LIDDELL, who comes in quite suddenly, UL, her face flushed. She is surprised but relieved by the scene that greets her.)

MRS. LIDDELL: *(To herself)* Thank God . . .

DODGSON: *(Standing, embarrassed to be caught in his shirt sleeves)* Why, Mrs. Liddell . . . good afternoon.

MRS. LIDDELL: *(Coldly)* Go along now, Alice. The other girls are waiting for you outside. You are all going to the marionette show.

ALICE: But we were going to have an unbirthday party.

MRS. LIDDELL: Not today.

ALICE: But Uncle Dodgson has a new story about . . .

MRS. LIDDELL: No. Run along now.

ALICE: *(Turning to* DODGSON, *disappointed)* I'm sorry, Uncle Dodgson. Don't forget about the Snark, so you can finish telling me next time.

DODGSON: I won't. The next time I see you I shall have the whole story for you. Even the part with the . . . *(Conspiratorially)* . . . boojums!

ALICE: Promise?

DODGSON: Promise.

(ALICE *kisses him on the cheek and runs out.* MRS. LIDDELL *flinches at the show of affection.)*

DODGSON: *(Looking after* ALICE*)* I won't get out of that one, I'm afraid. Alice never lets one off a promise. *(Then, noticing* MRS. LIDDELL's *chilly demeanor)* Is . . . something wrong, Mrs. Liddell?

MRS. LIDDELL: Yes, Mr. Dodgson. Something is very wrong. Very wrong indeed.

DODGSON: Not more rumors about Miss Prickett and myself, I trust.

MRS. LIDDELL: It has nothing to do with Miss Prickett.

DODGSON: *(The seriousness of the matter beginning to dawn on him)* I am at your service, madam.

(Pause)

MRS. LIDDELL: From this moment forth, you are not to set foot over the Deanery threshhold. You are not to speak with my daughters, or write to them, or communicate with them in any way—is that understood?

DODGSON: *(Appalled)* Mrs. Liddell . . . !

MRS. LIDDELL: I am to blame for this as much as anyone . . . if only I hadn't been so *naive* . . . You were kind to them, and they were so fond of you. How was anyone to know what kind of a man you really were?

DODGSON: Kind of man I . . . ? Mrs. Liddell, I . . . I'm completely at a loss to understand what it is you . . .

MRS. LIDDELL: *(Turning on him)* Are you, Mr. Dodgson?

DODGSON: It *does* have to do with Miss Prickett—

MRS. LIDDELL: For the last time, it does *not*.

DODGSON: Then, what are we talking about?

MRS. LIDDELL: Alice, of course!

DODGSON: Alice?

MRS. LIDDELL: All the times you walked with her, took her picnicking and boating, never did I dream your attentions could be . . . *(Repulsed by the word)* . . . unnatural . . .

DODGSON: Unnatural?

MRS. LIDDELL: She is more to you than a little girl, isn't she? You've held her hand as if you were merely a friend, but your true feelings are quite different. You want to touch her, hold her, kiss—

DODGSON: No! Mrs. Liddell! I . . . I swear to you . . . m-my love for Alice is p-purely . . . purely . . . you have no right to make these unspeakable accusations!

MRS. LIDDELL: Surely a mother has a right to protect her child . . . !

DODGSON: But there is no justification . . .

MRS. LIDDELL: Is there not, Mr. Dodgson? Is there not? *(Takes photographs from her pocket and hands them to* DODGSON.*)*

DODGSON: *(Looking at them)* Surely you knew of these . . .

MRS. LIDDELL: Are you mad?

DODGSON: But Miss Prickett . . .

MRS. LIDDELL: Miss Prickett has been dismissed. I was brought these by a colleague of yours. He said they had been circulating among the students.

DODGSON: My God . . .

MRS. LIDDELL: When I think of you, alone with them, alone with my babies . . .

DODGSON: *(Sinks to the settee in shock)* Oh my God!

MRS. LIDDELL: Give them to me.

(She takes the photos from him and tears them up.)

MRS. LIDDELL: Give me your word that you will do the same to any others that may exist. Your word, Mr. Dodgson!

DODGSON: *(Weakly)* Yes . . . anything you say . . .

MRS. LIDDELL: If it were not for the scandal that would ruin their lives, I would have you publicly denounced. As it is, I dare not even tell my husband.

DODGSON: It was innocent . . . I swear . . .

MRS. LIDDELL: God will be the judge of that. Look to your scriptures, Mr. Dodgson: "When I was a child, I spake as a child, but when I became a man I put away childish things. For now I see through a glass darkly, but then face to face." May God have mercy on you.

(She exits UL. DODGSON *stands unmoving for some moments—then his eyes fall on the photographs and glass plate negatives on the desk. He crosses to them slowly, and, keeping his word to* MRS. LIDDELL,

tears the photos one by one, more and more anguished as he destroys all that he has left of ALICE.

When the photographs lie in scraps at his feet he begins to cry.)

DODGSON: No . . .

(He take the glass plates and hurls them to the floor smashing them.)

DODGSON: No!

(He sweeps the manuscript of Through the Looking Glass *off his desk—the pages scatter across the room—he knocks the toys and inventions off the desk. Then his eye falls on a gold-framed portrait of* ALICE *on the desk, He picks it up lovingly.)*

DODGSON: Alice . . . Alice . . .

(He clutches the picture to his chest . . . then realizes what he's doing.)

DODGSON: *(In horror) No!*

(He holds the picture away from him, his face contorted with pain.)

DODGSON: It can't be true! *(He looks for some help—to keep from going mad—there is none)* God help me!

(He is suddenly confronted by his own reflection in the looking-glass—mad-eyed, weeping, clutching the picture of Alice.)

DODGSON: *(A scream that tears from him)* No!

(With a single, violent gesture, he hurls the portrait at the looking-glass. Blackout.

From the darkness, the sound of shattering glass, as of a thousand mirrors breaking . . .)

[END OF ACT ONE]

Act Two

(Lights rise on DODGSON's *room. Compared to the way we last saw it, it now presents a barren—even sterile—impression. There is not a photograph, nor a toy, nor an invention to be seen; no remaining trace of the man who wrote* Alice in Wonderland. *The looking glass is gone.*

There is a knock on the door. When no one answers, it opens. DUCKWORTH, *holding the hand of a* LITTLE GIRL *of about eight, enters the room, followed by a nervous* HAYDEN, L. *Some years have elapsed. The little girl holds a copy of* Alice in Wonderland *and a shiny red apple.)*

HAYDEN: Now, Duckworth, we really shouldn't . . .

DUCKWORTH: Nonsense. He won't mind.

LITTLE GIRL: Where is he? Where's Lewis Carroll?

*(*HAYDEN *crosses R to make sure no one's there.)*

DUCKWORTH: He doesn't seem to be here just now, Agnes. I tell you what—why don't you go down and play in the garden, and I'll come and get you when he arrives.

AGNES: I don't want to wait in the garden.

DUCKWORTH: Go on downstairs.

AGNES: You won't forget to call me?

DUCKWORTH: I promise. Here. You'd best let Uncle Robinson hold onto your book for you. You don't want to get it soiled.

(She gives him the book and the apple and runs out.)

DUCKWORTH: *(Eating* AGNES' *apple)* I say . . . I expected a change, but nothing so drastic as this.

HAYDEN: Yes, he's a, ah, different man from when you last saw him.

DUCKWORTH: Yes, well, aren't we all?

HAYDEN: *(Amused at his eating the apple)* I must say, some things don't change.

DUCKWORTH: *(Acknowledging the friendship between them)* Thank goodness. What about Dodgson? He ever marry?

HAYDEN: Good heavens, no.

DUCKWORTH: *(Sits on DR edge of desk)* You're certainly being enigmatic about him, I must say. He does still write, doesn't he?

HAYDEN: Oh, yes, of course.

DODGSON: I always wondered that there was never another "Alice" book after the first two. Remember the day we read the first one in manuscript?

HAYDEN: Very well.

DUCKWORTH: *(Going around to back of desk)* It was right here in this room. I'd found it while snooping through his desk . . . *(He pulls on the drawer and it opens)* He can't have changed very much. Still leaves it unlocked. I say . . . *(Takes out a manuscript)* Look at his . . . must be his latest. *(Reads from the title page)* Symbolic Logic. Well, I suppose there might be a laugh in it somewhere.

HAYDEN: I'd leave it alone if I were you, old boy. He's not as tolerant as he used to be.

DUCKWORTH: *(Reading aloud)* "A Proposition of Relation, of the kind to be here discussed, has for its Terms, two Species of the same Genus . . . " Must be the way I read it.

(There is a noise from the hallway. DUCKWORTH *hastily crosses to the door to look out.* HAYDEN *crosses above desk.* DUCKWORTH *turns in a panic, tosses the manuscript, and the apple.* HAYDEN *slams them*

both into the desk drawer and closes it. DUCKWORTH *hooks to chair DR and sits.* HAYDEN *rushes to the door to greet* DODGSON. DODGSON *enters UL. There is a hesitancy in his movements to match the one in his speech. He looks as though he has not smiled in some time.)*

HAYDEN: Here you are, Dodgson.

DODGSON: Hayden. I w-wasn't expecting you, was I?

HAYDEN: Well, it being Commemoration and all . . . Look, here's Duckworth, come down from Edinburgh.

(DUCKWORTH *stands to greet* DODGSON. DODGSON *crosses to the corner of the desk, between them, awkward.)*

DODGSON: Oh. Duckworth. Yes.

DUCKWORTH: *(Jovially)* It *is* you! You know, when I heard them talking about "Reverend Dodgson", I thought they meant your father.

DODGSON: My f-father died last year.

(Embarrassed pause.)

DUCKWORTH: Oh . . . ah . . . I'm terribly sorry.

DODGSON: No need to be. He made his p-peace with God, as I have made mine.

(Awkward silence.)

HAYDEN: Ah . . . Duckworth and I were just on our way to the reception at the Deanery. Will we see you there?

DODGSON: I should think not, as I shan't be there.

DUCKWORTH: Why not, old man? Be like old times.

DODGSON: *(Sits at desk)* I do not go out on Wednesdays and I do not go to r-receptions. Now if you will excuse me . . .

DUCKWORTH: *(Crosses and sits on R corner of desk)* You know,

Dodgson, I've become rather a second-hand celebrity round where I live. Ever since my neighbors found out that I knew you, they never seem to tire of hearing me tell them about our little boating expedition to Godstow. I say Dodgson, could I ask you a favor? It won't take but a minute. I've brought my niece Agnes with me. She's been wanting to meet you and have you sign her book. *(Stands, crosses UL toward door)* She's waiting downstairs—I'll just have her come up then, shall I?

DODGSON: I think not.

DUCKWORTH: *(Turns back to* DODGSON*)* What do you mean?

DODGSON: *(Briskly)* I am constantly being plagued by people who feel they have a p-perfect right to invade my p-private rooms asking for autographs and such favors. If I had known what a Pandora's box it was going to be, I would never have let you persuade me to p-publish.

DUCKWORTH: But those books have sold thousands . . . they're classics!

DODGSON: If you gentlemen will excuse me, I have much work to do . . . *(He begins going through his notes)*

HAYDEN: *(Crossing to* DUCKWORTH, *trying to usher him out)* Yes, Duckworth, perhaps we'd better. Come along . . .

DUCKWORTH: *(Breaks away from* HAYDEN, *turns back to* DODGSON*)* Wait a minute. I know what this is—this is the pull-the-wool-over-old-Duckworth's-eyes, isn't it? It's all a joke! Oh, of course it is!

HAYDEN: Duckworth, I'm afraid . . .

DUCKWORTH: *(Laughing)* What a lark! You really had me going for a bit there, I must admit.

(DODGSON *hunts through the papers on his desk, finds the one he is looking for, and hands it to* DUCKWORTH)

DODGSON: This should convince you of my sincerity.

DUCKWORTH: *(Reading it)* "Mr. Dodgson is so frequently addressed by strangers on the quite unauthorized assumption that he claims the authorship of books not published under his name, that he has found it necessary to print this. He neither claims nor acknowledges any pseudonym or any book that is not published under his own name." *(Looking up, perplexed)* Surely . . . surely you can't deny that you're Lewis Carroll?

DODGSON: I can and I do. Good day, gentlemen.

DUCKWORTH: You . . . you really *mean* that?

DODGSON: *(Opening his drawer)* Yes. Now, if you'll excuse me . . .

(DODGSON pulls out his manuscript. DUCKWORTH's apple core rests on top of it. DODGSON begins to tremble with fury.)

DODGSON: Get out . . . both of you . . .

HAYDEN: *(Guiding him to the door)* I tried to warn you. Now, come along . . .

DODGSON: *Out!*

(They leave hastily. DUCKWORTH accidently leaves the copy of Alice *behind. Shaken and distraught, DODGSON paces the room furiously for some seconds. Then—his eye falling upon the book on his desk—he stops, his eyes riveted on it. Simultaneously attracted and repelled, he reaches hesitantly out to touch it. Picking it up in his trembling hands, he runs his fingers over its covers.*

Then, in a sudden, decisive gesture, he thrusts it into his desk, slamming the drawer closed. There is a knock at the door. He reacts in anger, thinking they have come back to annoy him further, until he hears GIBBS' voice.)

GIBBS' VOICE: *(Off)* Dodgson? Are you there?

DODGSON: *(Surprised)* Mr. Gibbs . . . ?

(GIBBS enters UL, not much changed from when we last saw him.)

DODGSON: Mr. Gibbs, what an unexpected p-pleasure.

GIBBS: Dodgson! How long has it been? So . . . these are your rooms, eh? Cosy . . .

(They sit in the two downstage chairs, GIBBS R, DODGSON L.)

DODGSON: What brings you so f-far from London?

GIBBS: I'm sorry I haven't visited you before, but the life of a publisher, you know. *(Sits)* I suppose you're going to say there's a moral to that, eh? *(No response)* Yes, well, I suppose I should get to the point . . . it's about your new book.

DODGSON: Yes?

GIBBS: Dodgson . . . you know of course that the last two mathematical textbooks of yours that we published have not been . . . how shall we say it? . . . among our top sellers.

DODGSON: Yes, but after all, they were intended for a scholarly readership rather than for the general public.

GIBBS: Yes, yes, quite. But, you must realize Dodgson, that MacMillan and Company is not a philanthropic enterprise. Now, a pair of books as phenomenally profitable as *Alice in Wonderland* and *Through the Looking-Glass* can, it is true, absorb the losses of quite a number of more specialized, scholastic works . . . but even that number, Mr. Dodgson, may be expected to have a limit.

(GIBBS rises.)

DODGSON: *(Also rising)* Mr. Gibbs, what is it exactly that you are t-trying to say?

GIBBS: *(Uncomfortably)* Well . . . to be perfectly blunt . . . I'm afraid we will be unable to publish your book on symbolic logic, or anything further of that nature that you may write.

DODGSON: Unable to . . . p-publish . . . ?

GIBBS: I'm sorry to be the bearer of unpleasant tidings, but you must understand our position.

DODGSON: But that's impossible. You said you would publish it. You *m-must* publish it!

GIBBS: Come, come, you haven't heard all that I have to say on the matter. We might be compelled to reconsider . . .

DODGSON: Yes?

GIBBS: . . . if you were to write another children's book.

(DODGSON's *spirits deflate, he backs up a step, then crosses US of desk.*)

GIBBS: Surely you could manage that easily enough.

DODGSON: No . . . n-no, I couldn't . . . it's quite impossible.

GIBBS: Then I fear that there is nothing more we can do for you.

DODGSON: *(Desperately, holding his manuscript)* Mr. Gibbs, please, can't we arrive at some c-compromise? I resigned my teaching duties some months ago to devote more of my time to study and to writing this manuscript. I have no other source of income.

GIBBS: It appears you should have planned your finances more wisely. But it can't be as bad as all that, can it? Unless I am mistaken, you continue to derive a modest profit from the sale of the Alice books, do you not?

DODGSON: Yes, but I have ceased to keep any of it for myself. I have several relatives who depend on my assistance . . .

GIBBS: Couldn't you resume your teaching duties?

DODGSON: No, no, I could never ask the D-Dean . . . it's quite out of the question . . .

GIBBS: Well, I'm sure you will be able to work something out. *(Going to the door, hesitating)* I'm sorry, Dodgson. Of course, if you change your mind about the children's book . . .

(GIBBS *exits.*)

(DODGSON *sits, staring numbly into space. BLACKOUT.*

From the darkness, the growing sound of conversation and other noises indicative of a social gathering. Lights rise on the Deanery filled with people, mostly young MEN *in their twenties. A few familiar faces can be seen as well: the* CHAPLAIN, *deep in conversation with a young* STUDENT; *and the* DEAN *himself, circulating around the room, shaking hands.* DUCKWORTH *and* HAYDEN *stand apart from the others, DR, the only ones who do not seem to be entirely enjoying themselves.)*

DUCKWORTH: Well, at least Agnes got to meet Alice. I had a devil of a time trying to explain about Lewis Carroll, though . . . probably because I don't understand it myself.

HAYDEN: I wonder if any of us ever will. Rather like him, actually, when you come to think about it . . . leaving us with an unanswerable riddle.

CHAPLAIN: *(Coming over to them)* Having a good time, gentlemen? I always do enjoy these occasions so.

(The CHAPLAIN *leads* DUCKWORTH *across L.* HAYDEN, *left alone on the sidelines, is surprised to see* DODGSON *surreptitiously enter the room.)*

HAYDEN: Dodgson! You came after all!

DODGSON: *(Embarrassed and nervous)* Y-yes . . .

HAYDEN: I say, this is wonderful. *(Calling into the crowd)* Duckworth!

DODGSON: *(Anxiously, quieting him)* Please . . . I d-don't want to intrude . . .

HAYDEN: Intrude? Nonsense. Everyone will be delighted to see you.

DODGSON: You don't understand. I've only c-come to see the Dean . . . on a business m-matter . . .

HAYDEN: Well, I'm afraid he's rather tied up with the festivities at the moment. Here, let me get some wine for you while you're waiting.

DODGSON: W-waiting . . . ? Oh, but I can't . . . it's very important that I see him immedi . . .

DUCKWORTH: *(Spotting him at last, joining them)* Dodgson! Thank God, you changed your mind. I don't mind telling you I was worried sick after we . . .

DODGSON: P-please . . . I don't have t-time for . . .

CHAPLAIN: *(Also joining them)* Why, my word, it's Reverend Dodgson! This is a distinguished occasion!

DODGSON: *(Seeing the DEAN, breaking away to him)* Dean Liddell! Thank goodness.

DEAN: Dodgson! Good heavens, man, what a surprise to see you here. One hardly ever catches a glimpse of you these days.

DODGSON: Sir, I n-need to speak with you, if I might . . .

DEAN: Yes, yes, of course. Lots to catch up on. Just let me get all this congratulatory nonsense out of the way and we'll have a nice long chat . . .

DODGSON: *(Looking anxiously around the room)* How soon will that b-be, do you think?

DEAN: Oh, not long. Another hour or so. *(Recognizing someone)* Ah, Hargreaves! Good of you to come . . . *(He moves off)*

(DUCKWORTH *and* HAYDEN *catch up to* DODGSON *again.*)

DUCKWORTH: I say, Dodgson, are you all right?

DODGSON: *(Nervously)* Yes, yes . . .

HAYDEN: You look pale as a sheet.

DODGSON: No . . . no, it's . . . vitally important that I speak to the Dean . . .

DUCKWORTH: You look ghastly.

HAYDEN: Is there anything we can do for you, old man?

DODGSON: No, please, it's nothing. I'll be f-fine. It's just that . . . this room . . .

(He starts to sway slightly. They quickly catch him by the arms, supporting him.)

HAYDEN: Something *is* wrong. Come along, we'll see you home . . .

DODGSON: *(Regaining some of his strength, shaking them off)* No! Please. Leave me alone. I'll b-be quite all right if everyone will just leave me alone!

DUCKWORTH: Yes. Of course. Come along, Hayden. Let's see how Agnes is getting along with her new friends . . .

(They disappear into the crowd.

DODGSON *is momentarily left alone on the outskirts of the activity. He takes a deep breath, trying to compose himself. A young* STUDENT *tentatively approaches him.)*

STUDENT: Excuse me . . . Reverend Dodgson?

DODGSON: Y-yes?

STUDENT: *(Shaking his hand)* Allow me to tell you, sir, how very much I've enjoyed your books.

DODGSON: *(Guardedly)* Why . . . thank you.

STUDENT: They were a great help to me in getting through my math boards.

DODGSON: *(Warmly)* Indeed? This is really m-most gratifying. These would be the *Curiosa Mathematica?*

STUDENT: Why, no sir. *Alice in Wonderland* and *Through the Looking-Glass.*

DODGSON: B-but you said . . .

STUDENT: All I had to do was remember that the four functions of arithmetic are really Ambition, Distraction, Uglification and Derision to put it all in perspective.

DODGSON: *(Weakly)* I . . . I b-believe I *will* return at another time . . . excuse me . . .

(He starts for the door, but a SECOND STUDENT *blocks his path.)*

SECOND STUDENT: I beg your pardon . . . Lewis Carroll?

DODGSON: N-no! D-D-Dodgson!

SECOND STUDENT: I can't tell you how honored I am to meet you, sir. I've known both the Alice books by heart since I was ten.
(Reciting) "The Walrus and the Carpenter
  Were walking close at hand:
 They wept like anything to see
  Such quantities of sand . . . "

(The verse is picked up and echoed by various other guests overlapping in an impressionistic round.)

DODGSON: *(Looking around desperately)* I'm sorry . . . I m-must go . . .

THIRD STUDENT: *(Having overheard, coming over)* I say . . . *Through the Looking-Glass*, isn't it?

SECOND STUDENT: Not only that—this is Lewis Carroll!

DODGSON: N-no . . . please . . .

THIRD STUDENT: Lewis Carroll! By Jove!

OTHER STUDENTS: *(Hearing the name and gathering around; ad lib)* Lewis Carroll? . . . I say . . . good show . . . let's hear something . . .

DODGSON: *(Surrounded, panicking)* Really . . . p-please . . . I can't . . .

STUDENT: Do "Jabberwocky"!

OTHERS: *(Ad lib)* Yes, yes . . . "Jabberwocky" . . .

STUDENT: *(Ad lib)* Yes, please do "Jabberwocky"! . . .

(DODGSON *puts his hands over his ears as their clamor grows. Suddenly the sound is silenced as they all freeze.* ALICE—*still eight years old, still looking as she always did— runs across the stage and disappears into the crowd. No one notices her but* DODGSON, *who reacts as if slapped. He runs after her, breaking through the crowd, but she is gone.)*

DODGSON: Alice!

(The crowd moves aside and he turns and see her again standing DL with her back to him.)

DODGSON: Alice?

(She turns to look at him, then walks slowly away into a crowd of party guests. He follows her slowly—as he gets to the crowd, they move away one by one but ALICE *is not among them. Finally all the guests have moved away but the last one—*

A young woman in her late teens. She looks very surprised to see him.)

WOMAN: Uncle Dodgson?

(He turns to her . . . not knowing her. He is about to turn away.)

DODGSON: Excuse me . . . I . . .

WOMAN: Don't you know me?

DODGSON: No, I'm afraid not.

WOMAN: I'm Alice.

DODGSON: No . . .

(The other guests all disappear and the two of them are alone in a pool of light DC.)

ALICE: It's been so long since I've seen you. I know, of course, how busy you've been. I didn't understand at first. I thought you were deliberately avoiding me. You know how children are. But now I realize there must be many things more important to a famous author than a little girl he used to know.

DODGSON: Please, I must . . .

ALICE: But I'm glad I finally got this chance to thank you. When I was a little girl you gave me a gift—two books named for me—but they weren't the real gift—they were your gift to the rest of the world. Your gifts to me were the golden afternoons, the unbirthday parties on the bank, the boating trip to Godstow. You were the one friend whose voice echoes across my childhood. All those times we had, I will always have and I thank you for that.

DODGSON: You . . .

ALICE: Yes?

DODGSON: You're not Alice.

ALICE: Not—?

DODGSON: You must excuse me . . .

ALICE: Uncle Dodgson, I know I must have changed a great deal, but . . .

DODGSON: Please!

ALICE: The last time we were together . . . you began a new story for me:
  "'Just the place for a Snark' the Bellman cried,
  As he landed his crew with care . . . "

DODGSON: Please . . . No!

ALICE: If I'm not Alice, how would I know that?

DODGSON: I don't know what you want . . . I can't . . . It's too late!

(MRS. LIDDELL *appears right.*)

DODGSON: No! It's . . . it's not what you think!

MRS. LIDDELL: *(Suddenly bellowing as* QUEEN OF HEARTS*)* OFF WITH HIS HEAD!

(The room is transformed into a bizarre sort of courtroom. The DEAN *and* MRS. LIDDELL—*as King and Queen of Hearts—presiding in two chairs L, the* CHAPLAIN—*as the White Rabbit—taking the role of bailiff standing behind them.)*

(The other GUESTS—DUCKWORTH, JENKINS, PRICKETT, HAYDEN—*have been turned into jurors and witnesses sitting in the jury box—a table laying top forward. Two chairs back to back C are the witness stand—behind—and the prisoners box—facing front.)*

CHAPLAIN: Silence in court! Silence in court!

DEAN: Bailiff, read the accusation.

CHAPLAIN: That the prisoner did willfully murder one Lewis Carroll!

JURORS: Aaah!

DODGSON: *(Sitting, stunned in the "prisoner's box")* No!

DEAN: Now the verdict!

CHAPLAIN: Not yet, not yet. There's a great deal to come before that!

MRS. LIDDELL: Call the first witness!

CHAPLAIN: First witness! The March Hare!

(Fanfare as JURORS *nudge each other down the line.)*

DUCKWORTH: The March Hare!

PRICKETT: The March Hare!

JENKINS: The March Hare!

(HAYDEN *at the R end of box, giggles and crosses up center to hop onto the witness stand.*)

MRS. LIDDELL: Give your evidence and don't be nervous or I'll have you executed on the spot.

HAYDEN: But where shall I begin?

DEAN: Begin at the beginning, and when you come to the end . . . stop.

JURORS: Aaah!

HAYDEN: Well, we were following his trail of books, you see, and we came upon him and his inventions, all quite useless and delightful.

DEAN: Ah, that's important. Mark that down.

JURORS: *(As they do so)* Mmmm!

HAYDEN: He thought up stories and told time by a watch that doesn't run. The only odd thing was he'd never even thought of marriage.

DEAN: I wish *I'd* never thought of it.

MRS. LIDDELL: *(To DEAN)* Off with your head!

HAYDEN: *(Crossing down to MRS. LIDDELL on his knees before her)* What I meant was, he wasn't much on the ladies.

MRS. LIDDELL: *(Standing)* That's what you *should* have meant. What do you suppose is the use of a man without any meaning? Even a joke should have some meaning, and a man's more important than a joke, I hope. You couldn't deny that if you tried with both hands. *(She sits again)*

JURY: Hear! Hear!

HAYDEN: Yes, your Majesty.

DEAN: If that's all you know about it, you may stand down.

HAYDEN: I can't go no lower. I'm on the floor as it is.

DEAN: Then you may sit down. Don't take your time.

HAYDEN: It isn't *my* time.

DEAN: Aha! Stolen!

MRS. LIDDELL: Off with his head!

(HAYDEN *scurries over to the jury box*).

CHAPLAIN: Next witness: The Duchess!

(MISS PRICKETT *rises behind the jury box as* CHAPLAIN *blows a fanfare.*)

DEAN: Give your evidence.

PRICKETT: Shan't!

DEAN: *(To* MRS. LIDDELL*)* You cross-examine the witness. It makes my head ache.

MRS. LIDDELL: *(Crossing to jury box)* Always speak the truth. Think before you speak. And write it down afterwards.

PRICKETT: I deny it.

DEAN: She's in a state of mind to deny something, only she doesn't know what to deny.

PRICKETT: He came to the nursery often.

THE OTHERS: Oooh.

PRICKETT: Many nights a week.

THE OTHERS: Oooh.

PRICKETT: But not to see me. Oh, no, thank you very much. It was Alice.

(*The* JURY *group counters out, revealing* ALICE *behind the jury box.* DODGSON *is stunned to see her there.*)

THE OTHERS: Alisssssss . . . . . .

PRICKETT: She's the one. Couldn't see enough of her. I've said enough. Let the facts speak for themselves.

(DODGSON *tries to reach her, but the* GROUP *closes in again, and* ALICE *disappears.* DUCKWORTH *sits in the witness chair, holding a tea cup and saucer.*)

DODGSON: Duckworth . . . stop this, can't you?

DUCKWORTH: *(To* MRS. LIDDELL*)* I beg your pardon, your Majesty, it all began with the twinkling of the tea.

DEAN: The what?

DUCKWORTH: Well, it began with the tea.

DEAN: Well, of course "twinkling" begins with a "t". Do you take me for a dunce?

MRS. LIDDELL: What do you know about this man?

DUCKWORTH: Lewis Carroll was a very dear friend of mine. He knew about treacle wells and the proper rules of a caucus race . . . all the really important things. And now he's dead . . .

(DUCKWORTH *weeps copiously.*)

DODGSON: Duckworth, no! What are you saying? We made him up. We were drunk. He doesn't exist!

DUCKWORTH: *(Suddenly viciously to* DODGSON*)* He was killed by a cowardly little mathematician!

DODGSON: No! P-please . . . !

MRS. LIDDELL: The sentence! Pass the sentence!

DEAN: No, my dear. Verdict first. Then the sentence.

CHAPLAIN: He's already served the sentence.

MRS. LIDDELL: Sentence first, verdict after!

DODGSON: You c-can't do that!

MRS. LIDDELL: Why not? That's what you did. Condemned yourself on one witness's testimony.

DEAN: A witness who hadn't witnessed a thing. And a biased one, at that.

MRS. LIDDELL: Mothers are never biased!

DEAN: Next witness!

CHAPLAIN: Next witness: Charles Lutwidge Dodgson!

DODGSON: N-no . . . no, wait! I . . . I demand counsel!

MRS. LIDDELL: Counsel? No! Impossible! Never! *(Beat)* Oh, very well.

(JENKINS's *umbrella opens behind jury box.*)

CHAPLAIN: *(Crossing to the jury box with* DODGSON *in tow)* The Counsel for the Defense! The Counsel for the Defense!

(JENKINS *rises above the umbrella.*)

JENKINS: Here!

DODGSON: No! I p-protest this man's qualifications!

DEAN: Counsel, state your purpose.

JENKINS: To try the whole cause and condemn him to death.

MRS. LIDDELL: Qualified! Proceed!

JENKINS: *(Holding up a book)* Exhibit A!

DEAN: What is it?

JENKINS: A book, your Majesty.

(JENKINS *passes the book down the line to the King and Queen.*)

DODGSON: *(Trying to get the book back, failing)* Where did you get that?

JENKINS: It was found in the prisoner's room.

DEAN: Is it in the prisoner's handwriting?

JENKINS: No, it is not. And that is the queerest thing about it. It appears that he didn't write it after all.

DEAN: *(Finding several photographs inside)* Why, there are pictures inside.

JENKINS: Of course. What is the use of a book without pictures or conversations?

MRS. LIDDELL: *(Snatching photographs)* I'll take those!

DODGSON: No!

JENKINS: Are those pictures yours?

DODGSON: Yes, but . . .

JENKINS: Then you did write this book!

DODGSON: Y-yes . . .

JENKINS: But you have denied it!

DODGSON: *(Sitting back in his chair, shaken and confused)* It's only worthless n-nonsense . . .

MRS. LIDDELL: We'll see about that! Read!

DEAN: Read!

CHAPLAIN: *(Opening it and reading)*
"Twas brillig and the slithy toves
Did gyre and gimble in the wabe;"

MRS. LIDDELL: The most sensible thing I ever heard!

DEAN: Any further questions?

JENKINS: Only one, your Majesty. *(Glares down at DODGSON)* Who are you?

ALICE: *(Appearing from beneath JENKINS's umbrella as he steps down)* Alice, so please your Majesty.

DODGSON: No!

(DODGSON tries to go to her, but DUCKWORTH holds him back.)

DEAN: What do you know about all this?

ALICE: Nothing.

MRS. LIDDELL: Nothing whatever?

ALICE: Nothing whatever.

DODGSON: Alice.

JENKINS: *(Slipping her the umbrella, whispering)* One side makes you taller.

DODGSON: No, don't take it.!

ALICE: *(Nibbling at it)* It wasn't his fault. I asked him to tell me a story. *(She begins to slowly rise up off the stand)*

DODGSON: No!

MRS. LIDDELL: You will stop growing at once!

ALICE: I can't help it.

MRS. LIDDELL: You've no right to grow here!

ALICE: Don't be silly. We're all growing.

DEAN: Yes, but at a reasonable pace—

DODGSON: Alice, please! The *other* side!

(As she partakes, JENKINS umbrella hides her just long enough for her to be replaced by OLDER ALICE, who closes the umbrella.)

DODGSON: No! That's not Alice!

MRS. LIDDELL: How do you know?

JENKINS: When was the last time you saw this "Alice"?

DODGSON: The ... the twenty-third ...

DEAN: Aha! Ten years ago!

OTHERS: *(Ad lib)* Six years. Twenty years. Twelve years.

(Ghostly laughter echoes across the courtroom.)

DODGSON: What?

DUCKWORTH: *(Checking his watch)* Yes. Seven months, and sixteen days—

DODGSON: It can't be.

DUCKWORTH: Three minutes and fourteen seconds. Or ten if you're in a hurry.

MRS. LIDDELL: Then she was more to you than a little girl!

DODGSON: No!

MRS. LIDDELL: You wanted to touch her!

PRICKETT: Hold her!

OTHERS: Kiss her!

DODGSON: No! It's not true!

CHAPLAIN: How do you plead?

DODGSON: Innocent!

ALL: Innocent?

MRS. LIDDELL: We'll see about that! Jury?

DODGSON: No! You can't judge me! You don't know the first thing about it! Of course, I'm the only witness! *(Takes the stand himself speaking in a sporadic burst of speed, punctuated by stops, frantic, out of his head)*

DODGSON: *(Continuing)* She ran into the room looking for a disappearing cat . . . and she turned my pocket handkerchief into a mouse . . . a recitation—learn your grammar. Never stammer. Bread and butter. Never stutter. Kill canaries. Believe in fairies, and gypsies and mermaids and jaws that bite and claws that catch! No! That's not right . . . no . . . you've got to study hard because if you lose a second a day, you won't come right again for—sixty—sixty—twenty-four—three sixty five—for a hundred and eighteen years—that's right! You've got to be quick—to stay in one place—to do six impossible things before breakfast . . . No! Everything's coming out backwards: clocks, books, time, tea parties, and don't set foot over the Deanery threshhold! Or speak to her! Or write to her! And I didn't! I swear! I'm innocent! It wasn't a real mouse . . . just a pocket handkerchief . . . *(He pulls out his handkerchief but can no longer make it into a mouse)* . . . look . . . that's all there was . . . all the rest . . . all the unspeakable accusations are in your minds!

MRS. LIDDELL: Ha! That's all *you* know about it! *We're* all in *your* mind!

DODGSON: Then I deny you! You don't exist! You're nothing but a pack of cards! I made you up! I created you!

MRS. LIDDELL: You?

JENKINS: Who are you?

ALL: *(Advancing toward him)* Who are you?

DODGSON: I'm . . . I'm . . .

ALL: Yes?

DODGSON: I'm . . .

(DODGSON *staggers off the chair, taking a few steps downstage.*)

DUCKWORTH and HAYDEN: *(singing faintly in distance)* Lewis Carroll is my name . . .

DODGSON: No!

CHAPLAIN: Charles Lutwidge Dodgson! You have been found innocent of the charges for which you have already served the sentence.

MRS. LIDDELL: Which leaves *no justification*—

CHAPLAIN: For the murder of a perfectly delightful fellow!

DODGSON: It's too late . . .

HAYDEN: *(Turning back into himself)* Your photographs were beautiful and your inventions—well you really woke things up a bit in old Tom Quad.

DUCKWORTH: *(Taking off top hat)* You were bloody wonderful, old man. You made a marvelous impression on us. That's the important thing.

OLDER ALICE: Your gifts to me were the golden afternoons, the boating trip to Godstow . . .

ALICE: *(Appearing behind him)* Uncle Dodgson, I thought you left without saying goodbye.

(DODGSON *collapses, unconscious, downstage.*)

CHAPLAIN: Charge!

ALL: The murder of Lewis Carroll!

CHAPLAIN: Verdict!

ALL: Guilty!

(BLACKOUT.

Lights rise on DODGSON'S *room.* DODGSON *sits motionless on a chair, a shawl over his legs, his eyes looking inward, submerged in his own private grief.*

HAYDEN *has just brought in a tray of tea things and set it on the table behind* DODGSON, *who doesn't see him.* DUCKWORTH *hangs back near the door, uncertainly.)*

HAYDEN: *(Gently)* Dodgson? It's me old man. *(No response)* The doctor said it might be good for you to see some old friends . . . and we were all so worried about you . . . that . . . well, Duckworth wanted to look in on you before he goes back to Edinburgh. Would that be all right?

(No response.

HAYDEN *nods to* DUCKWORTH.*)*

DUCKWORTH: Well, you gave us all quite a scare, you know, collapsing at the Deanery like that.

HAYDEN: I'll say.

DUCKWORTH: One minute you were saying something about Alice and the next you were out cold just like that. I just felt a bit, well . . . responsible barging in on your privacy and bringing up a lot of old . . .

(HAYDEN shakes his head "no".)

DUCKWORTH: Well, I am sorry.

HAYDEN: *(To DODGSON)* You look a bit tired, old man.

DUCKWORTH: *(taking the hint)* Yes. And Agnes is waiting for me outside. So I'd best be off. Good-bye, Dodgson. Take care of yourself, won't you, old man?

HAYDEN: *(To DUCKWORTH)* I'll be along in a moment—wait for me.

(DUCKWORTH leaves.)

HAYDEN: Would you like me to open the window before I go? It's the first real spring day we've had all season.

(He goes to the window and opens it.)

HAYDEN: Another winter behind us . . . . You used to carry on so about the seasons, the passing of time. Seems you always had some new scheme for stopping it. But perhaps it always does win out in the end. Perhaps it's best to leave the past where it is . . . to carry on, you know? Worry about today . . . tomorrow . . . next week. That's enough for anyone without having to bear the burden of time gone by . . . Well . . . if there's anything you need . . . anything at all, you know where I am. You can look for me to come round for tea on the fifteenth, as always. I'll just look at my broken-down old watch, and when it's right . . . I'll know it's time. *(He puts a hand on* DODGSON's *shoulder)* Good-night, old friend.

(DODGSON's *hand moves up across his chest toward* HAYDEN's *hand, but before their hands meet,* HAYDEN *is gone without seeing it.* HAYDEN *exits L.*

A shadow flickers across DODGSON's *eyes.*

After a moment AGNES DUCKWORTH *pokes her head in.)*

AGNES: Have you seen my Uncle?

DODGSON *doesn't seem to hear her. She comes up to* DODGSON *directly.)*

AGNES: I said, have you seen my Uncle?

(DODGSON *looks at her, troubled and confused.)*

AGNES: I was waiting in the garden and he got lost. He often does. I have to keep an eye on him.

DODGSON: *(Murmurs, his eyes on her)* Alice.

AGNES: No. My name is Agnes. Are you having something good for tea? *(She crosses behind table to peek under the napkin.)*

DODGSON: Just . . . bread and butter.

AGNES: Oh. We're having cakes and jam . . . if I ever find Uncle Robinson.

DODGSON: Oh, you're sure to do that . . . if you look far enough . . .

AGNES: *(Smiling, crossing back to him DR)* The Cheshire Cat.

DODGSON: What?

AGNES: That's what the Cheshire Cat said. In *Alice*. It's my favorite book. Do you know Lewis Carroll?

DODGSON: I . . . I don't know.

AGNES: Oh, if you did, you'd know. He's famous. *(Pause)* Well, I'd better find Uncle Robinson. We're going to meet Lewis Carroll before tea.

(She crosses behind the table toward the exit UL. She is almost gone when his voice stops her.)

DODGSON: *(With tremendous effort)* Wait . . .

(She turns back to him.)

DODGSON: . . . I . . . am . . . Lewis . . . Carroll . . .

AGNES: You are?

DODGSON: Yes . . . I am.

AGNES: *(Eyeing him uncertainly, pause)* Prove it.

DODGSON: *(Remembering with pain and difficulty)*
    The . . . uh . . . "the walrus and the carpenter
    Were walking close at hand . . . "

AGNES: I know that and I'm not Lewis Carroll.

DODGSON: *(Pleased)* How very logical. What a bright girl you are.

AGNES: If you're really Lewis Carroll, tell a new story.

DODGSON: *(Troubled)* I . . . I can't . . .

AGNES: *(Disappointed)* I thought not.

(She pauses, then slowly starts to leave when he begins hesitantly.)

DODGSON: *(Going deeply into the past for a way to keep her there)*
    Just . . . the place for a snark . . .
    The Bellman cried . . . as he landed his crew with
      care.

(*AGNES stops and turns back, her interest piqued.*)

DODGSON: Supporting each man on the top of the tide
          By a finger entwined in his hair.

(*He glances up for a moment—sees that she has not gone, then goes back into himself, making up the next lines.*)

DODGSON: 'Just the place for a Snark! I have said it twice:
          That alone should encourage the crew.
          Just the place for a Snark! I have said it thrice . . . '
          'What I tell you three times is true.

(*She slowly begins to cross to him.*)

DODGSON: 'They sought it with thimbles, they sought it with care;
          They pursued it with forks and hope . . .
          They threatened its life with a railway share:

(*AGNES giggles.*)

DODGSON: They charmed it with smiles and soap . . .

(*She smiles at him, putting a small hand on his shoulder. He reaches out for her and pulls her to him, hugging her, choking with the enormity of his emotion. Lights fade quickly to BLACK.*)

[END OF PLAY]

www.ingramcontent.com/pod-product-compliance
Lightning Source LLC
Chambersburg PA
CBHW071733040426
42446CB00012B/2348